About the Author

Magdalena Lovejoy is a spiritual teacher and philosopher who communicates a true and deep faith to people from all walks of life. She writes with vision and clarity of the greatest philosophers and imparts simple, yet profound wisdom in her message: you can know your true self and be set free from suffering. She teaches her philosophy in her counselling practice to help clients attain happiness.

To Julie,

Five Ways of the Wise
A Guide to Freedom and Self-Mastery

*Here is a special gift
signed by the author for
your birthday. May you
have health, happiness and
many blessings for your life.*

Maydalena Torrejis

Magdalena Lovejoy

Five Ways of the Wise

Olympia Publishers
London

www.olympiapublishers.com
OLYMPIA PAPERBACK EDITION

A CIP catalogue record for this title is
available from the British Library.

ISBN: **978-1-78830-520-4**

The opinions and sentiments expressed in this work are
those of the author and not the publisher

First Published in 2020

Olympia Publishers
Tallis House
2 Tallis Street
London
EC4Y 0AB

Printed in Great Britain

Dedication

This book is dedicated to my son Zechariah, and to all those who touched my heart in my own soul-searching. These are all the things I think you need to know.

Acknowledgements

I wish to thank my first guru Swami Vagishananda Saraswati and I would like to express my gratitude to the Creator for inspiring me and for giving this book light and life.

Contents

Preface

This book is the result of almost twenty-five years of research in philosophy and spiritual practice. In the West, I studied in Canada; while in the East, I studied in the jungle of Bali, Indonesia. I went through initiations to attain my degree of enlightenment and various rites of passage. I would like to tell you briefly how this book came to be.

I was deeply troubled my whole life, constantly seeking deeper truths in order to be set free from an intense suffering that filled me with agony, grief, sadness, pain, and self-hatred during my early life. I had suicidal thoughts. I was filled with a deep pain about lostness. When I was in my late twenties, I followed a dream to go to Bali, Indonesia, where I attended my first yoga retreat. This was part of fulfilling my desire to be healed from life-long suffering. I met my guru at the yoga retreat. His name is Swami Vagishananda Saraswati. I eagerly sat before him and listened as he transferred the knowledge of the ancient Vedas and the Bhagavad Gita to the group when I heard him talk about my true identity as being pure, perfect, full, whole, and complete and my being pure, unconditional love. At once, I perceived myself as a separate entity, and a light came on within my mind. As I witnessed my mind, I said to myself, "that is my rejected and abandoned self, but I am not this; *I am that*," and I awakened to being the truth of who Swamiji said I was, which is the truth of who I really am. I saw the truth for what it is. I observed myself within an inner space of silence, and this space was God. I realized the truth of time and space. In the space of awareness, you and I are one. Within this inner space, I was in a deep, immoveable peace that surpassed all understanding, as Jesus claimed existed. It was pure stillness. There was no more suffering. I perceived that I was the light shining behind the mind as pure witness awareness, and that light was God. I perceived the Tree Of Life within me and sensed that all of God's creatures were in my space, sharing in oneness. The truth I realized was in the depth of my Being. I perceived that I was the space of awareness that observed the pain and suffering of the entity called the ego as a projection in time and space and as separate from the truth of who I really was. I thought to myself that everything is a projection, but I was independent of this projection. I realized the entity that I lived with my whole life was not real. Therefore, everything I conceived about myself was not real. It was as if a dream created by language. I realized this entity within me stood against love and only wanted to die, but I didn't want to die. I wanted to live fully. I felt something powerful that day with my guru. His words resonated within my deep self. This light that came on that day continued to burn for truth in my devotion.

During the yoga retreat, Swamiji taught us to imagine putting a flower to the heart and to see it blossoming within your heart. Awakening, as I understood it, was the inner flowering of consciousness. Here the blossoming flower is a symbol and the reason for the cover photo on this book. I began collecting flowers for Swamiji and each day I gave him a flower to show my devotion. Each day I put a flower to my heart. I focused intensely on my heart consciousness to escape my mind, which I perceived filled with an evil. This evil put obstacles in my way continuously that I had to remove while I traveled on my path of love. I removed these obstacles through alchemy. Alchemy was the way of healing. Life is alchemy.

I had understood the knowledge from my training in philosophy. I could literally feel the light of truth shining to reveal the way within and the true Path. The darkness that hung over my head had lifted. I could see the light of God shining on my path. When I looked at the outside world, all people and creatures were enveloped in His oneness and all things were divine expressions of His love. I felt love coming out of my Being, touching and connecting me to the universe. I ascended into a higher world. Solitude is the ground of Being.

I gave my entire heart and soul to the transmission of these oral teachings. As a result of my faith in these teachings, I realized my self within three years, at the age of 29. This is called self-realization. I felt I existed inside the center of God's consciousness. I realized the truth that

Jesus was the pure, unconditional love that I believed to be myself, and He was pure, perfect, full, whole, and complete, and so was I. I became a born-again Christian and attained enlightenment after hearing that I was the way, the truth, and the life, like Jesus.

I perceived a deep truth; each spiritual master was teaching the same truths, although their essential teachings were covered up. Where I quote from ancient religions, this is intended to restore their truth and transform you from within.

This book is a direct transmission of hearing the truth from God. At the heart of this book is its power to draw your attention to the dichotomy between the true and false selves so that you will experience an awakening. This awakening is not possible unless you can perceive the nature of what is true and what is false within you. Touching the heart, you will discover the inner person. This is why I reveal the ancient truths to you. They will deeply resonate within your Being and help you recover the power that is held in knowledge. Powerlessness comes from ignorance. By recovering this knowledge, you can be healed and transformed.

The most powerful practice I learned was a self-discovery method of search. It is extraordinarily powerful and effective at revealing the truth that all people desire to attain in their quest for enlightenment. It typically takes years of study to learn these truths, but here I have made awakening possible.

My own journey into self-development was guided by my desire to become whole. In healing my own wounds, I learned the path of compassion and discovered how to care for others. I actively learned to transform the pains and sufferings of grief, loneliness, sadness, shame, and guilt, into happiness, joy, wholeness, and health. At my philosophy counseling practice, I work with individuals to transform their soul wounds into self-empowerment using the dialogue of search.

The wisdom that I speak about is true to the sacred knowledge that I learned from my initiation and from my own transformation to becoming a self-realized being.

Love Magdalena

INTRODUCTION
The Messenger

There was once a pioneer who turned himself into a philosopher by seeking to become the love and the light that he had heard about. The pioneer was equivalent to the human being a long time ago. The reality that we have now is like the one that we find in the ancient mind. He had at his disposal the ways of magic and he knew how to live the life that we all dreamed of. He knew that he could transform himself using his mind alone. Alchemy was his element. This engineering that he knew he could do on himself was the power that he knew he had within. When he came into contact with other human beings, he found that there were none like him. He was a messenger. He found his messages in the magic he filled his life with. He found that when he spoke the ancient ways of the mystics, his language could create an eternity. He proclaimed with his own voice, "I am that," and that was the boundlessness that he called love. And from this awareness, he could also say, "And you are what I am." With this realization, he attained an inner sense of freedom from everything that had disturbed him before. The words were not from him, but they were from another dimension. The words he used could pronounce the syllables of life. He believed in something called truth. He realized that this is the language that is in the minds of all people so all people could know the ways of the wise when he spoke the language of truth. Living with other people, he realized that they did not follow the same path. He proclaimed to people, "There is a chance to be greater than you are; so, follow me. I am The way, The truth, and The life." And people from all around stopped and listened to his words.

He would build himself a refuge until he knew that he himself was the refuge and that building was not something external, but an internal way of creation. He set himself upon a stone and turned that stone into liquid through the alchemy of the way of the ancients. So, it was knowledge that brought him to the point of self-dissolution. This was the way of understanding who you truly are, he realized. What was once lead could be turned into liquid gold by understanding that your soul is eternal. He who set himself on this truth erected a building called love that no man could dissolve. This took him into purity because truth was beyond the limitations of the mind. When he realized that he was pure, he realized he was also perfect, full, whole, and complete. The alchemist learned he was shining bright in the world. When he realized that life was shining through his eyes, and that he was the light himself, and that all of life declared a truth of God, he said, "Heaven is here to be realized by all beings." He found that these five aspects were the ways of a great truth of our original nature. And then he realized that this was his essence that he could contain. And it was a pure essence like fire. This, he believed, could build the greatest foundation for the soul. What one man needs to do is work on himself, and another needs to deny himself. He began to alchemize this understanding, from lead into gold. This was the secret that he told only to a few people, and he needed to know why the people were so far away from him. So he asked himself, where did this purity come from? The answer was from a great stone. This stone was called the philosopher's stone. It had within it the power of alchemy. He could transform his inner world into a god. This is what they called him, God, when they found that he was acting like God. And he said that his godlike space was their space as well. They too were God. He believed that each person had an original nature and he said to each one, "You are pure, perfect, full, whole, and complete." This was the way of God seeing God.

This is what he realized. "Truth is the way that you can attain mastery. It has within it the power to show you the world. What it shows you is that there is an illusion and there is truth. The illusion is that you are incomplete, imperfect, and empty. The way shows you the opposite. You are pure, perfect, full, whole, and complete. This is your original nature and true form. These are the five aspects of your true self that is rooted in Being. They teach you to become whole again so that you can be truly who you are. I am here for you." He realized that the waves of reality cannot get him anymore because he was set apart from the illusion. He thought to himself that there are so many things with the number five that this number has great meaning. He who discovers the five aspects within himself is touching upon the ways of God. "Your perfection is God's perfection," the alchemist said. "This is the true reality of light." He said, "You are not your body. You are not your mind. You are the truth of everything. Here is your Being. The love that you feel in my eyes is the truth of the love that you are. The impurities cannot come into contact with what is pure and eternal. This is the greatness of your eternity." You will say, 'This is who I was, and this is who I am now.' He believed the five truths of his original nature touched upon an eternal reality, a way of the wise itself. He wanted to share this with all people, but his words fell upon deaf ears, yet they believed in his messages because he came to them in a true form. He declared, "The way that you thought you were is no longer here for you."

He became aware of many things after this realization. He found that there was a mirror in himself. This produced the space of existence that he called love. The mirror showed him that he was love. When the alchemist finds his heart, he has cosmic awareness. This gives him the opportunity to know that he is the stars, the moon, the sky, the trees, the sun, and the mountains. And he has the awakening that his heart is within the heart of all. This leads him into the purest state of existence, one in which no one can tarnish his truth. It is the truth within all people that he could perceive, that they too are like him, with these five qualities of their Being. But few people could understand that he has this purity. It is as if their minds have been identified with the impure for too long. This was the power of the illusion. He showed them the universe was a manifestation of their truth, but still the truth wasn't understood. "When you turn within your own self," he said, "you will see that I am there, and the truth of my nature is the truth of you being present with yourself. For our image of light is the same. We are reflections of the divine." The mirror within himself reflected this truth of love to all people, and their spiritual eyes were opened. The illusion fell away from the people he spoke to and the dream that clouded their reality was lifted.

Here you can know the space of existence is really like a mirror. This has a dream-like appearance in it. In all things, you can be what appears. There is a phenomenon of magic. Little by little, you can take from the mirror and look into the glass when you are down. Did you ever feel that your hope for yourself was meaningless? When you find out there is nothing to be afraid of, because it is what is appearing before your life, you can find that there is a way of Being. This mirror is the consciousness of all humankind. It talks to the brain differently by showing that there is something of a phenomenon, and when you find this phenomenon, you can find it has the essence of Being in it. Did you ever want to say, "I am not this"? Of course, you did. When you find out you can be almost anything you want, this can be the light on your course. Can you take the mirror for granted? Of course, you can. The mirror says to you, these are the ways of the wise. This mirror can be positioned in your life so that you can find the ways more clearly. When you say something to yourself, there is a mirror that says, it is real or it is not real. The truth of the ways of the wise is that they are alive in the consciousness of humankind. When you find yourself failing, you know you need a mirror to show you the truth. Having the truth in mind is not popular, and often those who are compelled to speak it are unpopular. You can use an affirmation like "I like myself" against the smoke and mirrors to show that it has a consciousness that is alive. This takes you into a greater space of existence, one in which you can say, "There is life." The mirror places your soul right.

When the alchemist dies to his old self and the old patterns fall away, he will not be looking to the outside world to manifest his desires anymore. He finds the inside world greater with truth. This is his soul's yearning to discover how to be alive. The way of the inside world is not shaken anymore by the thoughts, judgements, and perceptions of others. This will give him a sense of authenticity. And the inner alchemy of his mind will not shut away his heart. This inner alchemy is the mind's undoing of the patterning of humankind so that he can start with a fresh canvas with which to paint his new self into creation.

When the alchemist sets his heart right, all the universes will be set right, because in essence they are one. For the truth of the alchemist is the truth of all people. The alchemist knew there was more to learn. He deepened his knowledge by listening to God reveal the ways of the wise. Each truth was shared by all people so that they could remember their original nature and go the way of the wise. He believed that once finding themselves, they would find God. "The truth is here for all people. How do you want to find your truth?" he said. Truth has the effect of allowing you to behold the supreme wisdom. With this self-consciousness that he uncovered in his alchemy, the five ways of the wise were given to him as the means to help people find their truth. The numerical significance within the way is bigger than this articulation. This story is what he learned by revelation. And the work that he did will be revealed clearly. It is special to receive the wisdom so clearly. All that you hear is from God. It is the will of the prophet.

Human Patterning and The New Program

What you are experiencing right now is part of your programming. During your whole life, you are programmed to believe certain things, say certain things, and behave in a certain way. The program is alive in all aspects of our lives. Even reading this book is part of your program. The program that we are part of is in human consciousness. It has to do with our waking life. But we fail to realize that we are programmed because the way of reality is made up of dreams. You are the dreamer. A dream is an illusion that we must overcome. Only the truth is real. This old program will be deleted in the five ways of the wise, and a new program will be restarted in the Path of Freedom and Self-Mastery so that you can learn how to recover your Being. Your life can be restarted on the right path.

How long has it been since you last considered your life journey?

You can learn to live freely by following the five ways of the wise. Each way is an opportunity for global awakening. For the current state of humanity is about the coming of a Savior. There is a movement happening that will create a shift in your awareness so that you are awakened and the illusion is revealed. Why are the five ways so important? Because they are effortless in being a catalyst for freedom and human development.

Trust that you have found a maven in the ways of wisdom.

If you understand these five ways, you will understand what the Masters of life were saying, including Buddha, Moses, Christ, Krishna, and other Masters. Wisdom is a special aspect of truth of the Buddha. What they were saying didn't evoke controversy, and there is no difference. As you follow their wisdom, you can learn to be completely authentic in your Being. Being is the world within in the core of the multiplicity that is without connection to the mental states of existence that we call patterns of the self. It is undeniably the essence of who we are. This is a frontier of knowing who you are as an indivisible human being. It's a stillness within that is disguised with the thoughts. With this knowing, we take on a new access of awareness. In this way, there is no difference between you and any other Master. You can be who you truly are. You are unique. You cannot be anybody else. You are truth. There is a Being in you that is unalterable. You can only be what you are. But everything going through your mind is not truth. It is an illusion built up on the falsity of the outside dream.

Concerning the things of greatness, the truth be told, it was the spiritual Masters that knew the way. Being a traveler in life's journey is part of a great dream, but there is a truth that it is revealed in this metaphor. That truth is called the Path. The Eastern mystics wrote about this truth. They called it the way.

Confucius wrote in verse VII. B.16 of the Analects when he said, "Mencius said, 'Benevolence means "man".' When these two are conjoined, the result is the way." The way is implied in the metaphor "life is a journey". Here the way is thought to be something internal as well. This journey has, since the beginning of time, been linked to the ways of the wise. But the greatest journey is within. This is the world that cannot be shaken. "You have found your way" is a common linguistic saying that you will hear when people touch the ways of the wise. It's not a long way, but a true way. It can get you to the goal of self-realization, leaving behind the call to be different. Nothing is real but the way. This is the same way spoken of by Jesus in John 14:6 when he says, "I am the way, the truth, and the life." The same idea is expressed in Matthew 7:14: "Because strait is the gate, and narrow is the way, which leadeth unto life, and few there be that find it." The way is the truth of this book. Jesus found life to be worth living from the sheer fact that he could teach the way.

The way moves like the flow of a river with continuous movement and change, with waves, water ripples, tides, undulations upon the water surface, vortices and stillness. The Ashtavakra[1] Gita 15:11 says, "Let the waves of the universe rise and fall as they will.

---

[1] Ashtavakra Gita, translated by Bart Marshall.

You have nothing to lose. You are the ocean."1 The face of the one that observes the water is timeless. It goes forward to an infinity of duration. The patterns it produces are likenesses of Being. When we can find ourselves saying something to another person, we find this is a motion in the water. And the points of stillness that we can perceive are likened to the silence that we can attain. The way of nature, such as the winds, changes the face of the water. It produces shapes and patterns that are visible to the eye. This is the flow of how the way of Being is perceived in the way of the Tao through discernment. God has set forth the movement of the water to be like the movement of the stars. So, when we perceive it in ourselves, we can also perceive the cosmic evolution. Saying something to another person can stir the waters so deep that it can lead to perplexity. Deep within our Being, we have lost the way. This can be undone by stilling the mind. Looking out onto the surface of the water, one can see the motion has its cause in life. Here the heart has come into fruition. What can be known in the way can be known in your Being.

Life is like a stream. You are the image of the stream. Keep moving. You have the power to direct the flow to a destination, either toward bodily pleasures or toward truth. Your essence is flow. Feeling the flow is in the art of dialogue. It's in the unfolding of truth. You can never be unavailable to this flow, because it is where you are. For those held captive in the darkness of mental clutter, distraction, chaos, and illusion, freedom is movement toward truth, and away from ignorance. It's the life-principle that is realized upon the freeing of the prisoners, that what was once motionless is given motion in the very act of freedom itself. Can the movement ever really be discovered without you? It has within it the force to be self-realized. What was once motionless is given the motion by the seed of life. This is planted within your soul to allow you to come into Being. So never can you be outside this movement of life. It is you. Be a truth-seeker. You are the cause that brings about the truth of the soul.

Let it flow.

The Masters of life know intuitively that the five ways of the wise are a Path taken by all. As Buddha said in the Samyutta Nikaya, there is an "ancient Path" like an ancient road traversed by the rightly enlightened ones of former times. This is why at the conclusion of this book, you will find a path to freedom and self-mastery. In Proverbs 3:5-6, the way is shown with a path of life: "Trust in the Lord with all your heart, and do not rely on your own understanding. Acknowledge him in all your ways, and he will make your paths straight." Understanding the five ways of the wise is a way to self-realization. According to these sacred texts, you have already started out on this Path. You need to get clarity on your overall life-path so that you can take the next step. Taking into consideration the phenomenon of life, we can hear that there are different points of view everywhere, yet none is as clear as the world within. Truth is about the world within. The ways are not perceivable by any means. When you consider the five ways of the wise, you will have the chance to become akin to God. This is what Moses attempted when, in

Exodus 33:13, he said to God, "Show me now thy ways." And God showed them to him. In Psalm 103:7, it was written that God "made known his ways unto Moses".

Knowing the way wasn't effortless. He who went the distance with the Masters was regarded highly. It was as if his mind was an eternal existent gem shining for us to behold. The day the Masters knew something about life was the day humankind was set free. Walking a bit with these spiritual Masters will lift the masks that we wear in our social roles. The message of these Masters exists in the essential teachings. The light can get brighter with these teachings. The teacher is still present therein. It is still within reach of everyone searching for it. It is still radiant to this day. Your walk with the Masters on this planet is called the Earth Ancient Mystery School. How long have you been under the impression that there was a way? It is here that you will learn the sacred wisdom. Follow closely with your pen in hand. Heart can be lost, and finding your heart is the purpose of this story. Jesus and Buddha were setting people free with the same wisdom.

You can start your soul journey with this knowledge of the way.

We have come across the idea that reality is a dream in the sacred texts authored by spiritual Masters. Don't harden your hearts toward the greater eyes. These texts have the power to identify the illusion of the outside world with clarity and purpose. In Taoism, Zhuangzi says: "Once upon a time, I, Zhuangzi, dreamed I was a butterfly, fluttering hither and thither, to all intents and purposes a butterfly. I was conscious only of following my fancies as a butterfly, and unconscious of my individuality as a man. Suddenly I awoke and I lay, myself again. Now I do not know whether I was then a man dreaming I was a butterfly, or whether I am now a butterfly, dreaming I am a man."[2] He also wrote, "There is the great awakening after which we shall know that this life was a great dream. All the while the stupid think they are awake."[3] There was a Way in the texts of Zhuangzi, and he knew he could see through the illusion.

This spell that Zhuangzi wrote about is powerful enough that even Buddha considered it in his life. In the Diamond Sutra, Buddha says, "All conditioned dharmas are like dreams, illusions, bubbles, shadows, like dew drops and a lightning flash: contemplate them thus."[4] The way of Buddha is very common to all people. Understanding these texts is part of discerning the nature of things. Buddha had the way in an effortless mind. When you set your sight on something wise, you know that you will succeed.

In Advaita Vedanta in the Bhagavad Gita, it says, "Brahman Satyam Jagat Mithya," meaning Brahman is the real reality, the world is unreal and deceptive, because it is superimposed on Brahman.[5] This superimposition creates the illusion of the outside world. Truth takes the superimposition away. In the Chandogya Upanishad

---

[2] Zhuangzi's "Dream of the Butterfly," A Daoist Interpretation by Hans Georg Möller, *Philosophy East and West,* Vol. 49, No. 4 (Oct.1999), pp. 439-450
[3] "This is All A Dream," by Timothy Conway, 1983.
[4] Diamond Sutra, by Dhyana Master Hsüan Hua.
[5] Translating Myth, Ed. By Ben Pestell, Pietra Palazzolo, Leon Burnett.

verse 8.3.2 it says, "As one not knowing that a golden treasure lies buried beneath his feet may walk over it again and again, yet never find it, so all beings live every moment in the city of Brahman, yet never find him because of the veil of illusion by which he is concealed." This is the power of the philosophic nature in all of us, to discover what is beneath the veil of illusion. Love is the power to pierce through the veil.

The way the world works is that there is an illusion covering the truth. The veil puts us in a space of existence that we are not here. It hides our Being. This is what makes it seem as if it is normal for us to suffer. When the veil is lifted by the five ways of the wise, you can turn back the time to your childhood and recover your innocence, called your true self. The human predicament is that we have been trapped. The heart that knows the way can say to itself, "I am here."

When you see yourself for the first time, it is as if the butterfly does not have any wings. This is the quest of the philosopher. This is called transformation. The wisdom found within the sacredness of God does not lose anything when you have a way for transformation. You move from the illusion to truth. The way of the philosopher is what you want to recover.

But what is the philosopher? The word philosopher means "lover of wisdom". God set forth wisdom in the heart. You have a heart for wisdom when you are a philosopher. The philosopher can move his soul into higher worlds by contemplating both the changing and the unchanging, the harmony and the chaos, where the fruits of his knowledge will become eternally placed within the mind. The philosopher comes to know himself quicker than all other people and can dissolve the boundaries of the enemy so to create an equilibrium in his life. In essence, by transporting himself into a godlike state, by allowing reason to govern his thoughts, the ignorance of the world goes further and further away from the philosopher.

Love is the journey within.

In the planetary dimension, we aspire towards wisdom in phenomenal ways. We often find that even with the errors we make on a daily basis, there is a constancy in us to undo the ways of ignorance. We find that there is a god called Wisdom, and in all things the god makes the world unquestionably good. It is this goodness that we find in the five ways of wisdom. The seed of truth is undeniably in the knowledge of the difference between virtue and vice, for therein lies the power to go forward in life, and this knowledge makes possible the eternal union of the masculine and feminine parts of the psyche, who have found themselves to be separate, not out of their doing, but from an original separation, and this is the cause of the suffering. At the heart of wisdom is this ability to create the wholeness of Being. The truth be told, wisdom is about a self-governing society in their efforts to aspire toward greatness, thereby diminishing the face of the demon. In life, the times they are changing. Moreover, there is none like the self-governing person. For he has put virtue and vice correctly in the state of union. This allows this effort of love to triumph. The way within is of discernment of evil and good.

The search for wisdom is not effortless. The articulation of the five ways leads to knowing the supreme wisdom of the cosmos.

The philosopher is a Savior; he will save your soul from illusion, falsehood, error, and impurity. The philosopher will go down into the darkness of Hell and guide you to the light of the heavens. The five ways of the wise are within the soul for humankind. So be awake when God makes the move to show you the light. The five ways of the wise will lead you to God. They unfold by way of truth, and truth is God's light revealed. Believing the truth and searching for self-knowledge is the way of the light and the way to dissolve the spiritual darkness that comes from self- ignorance. When you choose truth, you choose the light instead of the darkness. The way is from darkness to light. The beginning was a philosophy, and so was the middle, and so was the end. That is why there can only be a dialogue of search. And what you are searching for is always the truth. Placing your heart in the philosophy is the way to attain self-mastery. When searching for wisdom, the wise person knows how to discipline himself with philosophy so that truth does not elude his grasp and he walks the correct path of life. The philosopher is the way of wisdom itself. It cannot go beyond his mind to know there is a purpose. It is the light within that inspires each question and that is an immeasurable, unsurpassable, incalculable searching for truth. When you awaken, the burden of Being will be shouldered by the confidence you feel within. Take heart. There are efforts being made to solve life's problems, including the wars we have with others and express within ourselves. The Buddha, too, proclaimed that he would save all beings and release them from their sufferings.

It is not too late to start the path of wisdom. He who fails to realize that it is the alchemy of the self-consciousness will fail to realize that the philosopher is the ultimate person. Just as you know yourself, you can also know the ways of the wise.

The illusion that we think we are living is nothing but a dream. It is the dream of "myself" that continues with reference to the truth of the way things are. The delusions of "me" and "mine" are what the program of human consciousness continues in our thinking. The sicknesses of society all come down to whether one is dreaming or staying conscious of one's mental awareness. The consciousnesses of the sicknesses of society fail to believe the truth. This can mean they are lacking in the faculties of human emotion; they can be without love. Life on planet Earth needs human emotion desperately to curb the effects of lostness. You are moving in the place of love where all the superimpositions of the ego are trying to hold you back from realizing the truth of love. Just sense the truth. This is even making a distinction between good and evil, for what is realized as good is love and what is realized as evil is the superimposition. You can feel the evil dissipate when you are in contact with the truth. This way, the world will not be able to project its mind. This will lead to the freedom and self-mastery that you wish to attain. This is a life worth living.

Knowing is half the battle.

What you have is a cloud in your mind if you do not know that oneness is possible. You need to start thinking consciously so that the cloud dissipates. You need to take hold of the reality behind the cloud. Holding onto your love is how you can do this. Love is the reality that you will encounter with each page-turning. Therefore, you will not fail. Even the whole world can come against your dream, but when you hold onto love, you will be immune to their programming. What the programming is trying to tell you is that the five ways of the wise is a conscious mechanism. It is something that responds to your belief, and it is something that can be channeled directly so that you can do the work of the alchemist. Holding onto this thought of consciousness is what we are all here to do. This learning is not without effort.

But what is consciousness? Consciousness is undefinable because it evades this type of knowledge. It's as if there can be light that shines, and you can say, "Here it is," and then it goes from you instantly. So, what you are attempting to be conscious of is the light, and it says, "It shines" in your mind; so your consciousness is your aliveness, and even this cannot be found to be within the base of knowledge. The knowledge of consciousness is as evasive as a dream.

Often your mental clutter stops the truth from manifesting into reality. You can realize truth when you consciously try to overcome the sicknesses of your mind. This can be your basis for overcoming the world. The program makes us wired for selfishness, greed and a lack of heroism. When we overcome, we transcend our suffering. We are addicted to suffering. The addictions that you have for yourself, like alcohol and over-eating, can send your truth into a different place where you will have to find the way to be set free. So, ending these addictions is what wisdom can do. The work that you can do in your own life can transcend all evils. This has to do with consciously moving your mind to a healthier and happier place where you triumph over the tragedies and find joy, and even bliss. When you transcend the suffering, you make your mind available to healthier dreams. These can be about your life eternal or your life abundant. There is nothing greater than finding the means within these ways to achieve. The means have to do with sorting out your life. What was once lost can be found.

So, you think that you have had enough pressure from life?

You have to see through the web of illusion and disentangle the true self by piercing the veil deep enough to say, "I am here." This book will teach you to disentangle your Being. The dream or illusion of the Buddha is the same as a facade. It has nothing real to it because the original form has been covered up by the old program. The illusion of the false self makes the illusory self-identifiable. In the nature of this illusion, there are a multiplicity of faces showing up to represent your sense of self. They comprise your thoughts of your childhood most deeply. It is as if the faces are your real self, but all they do is confuse you. It's a long way from knowing that you are a true self right now. The illusory self is also called the ego self. In your consciousness, you have the self that wants to be these faces. They cannot teach you what the intrinsic self is. The illusory self needs to be extinguished and your Being needs to be recovered. What the people could not see about themselves the alchemist could see, so that he could save them from the ocean of illusion by showing them, with his mirror, that they are like him. Life is full of illusions, believed the Buddha. This is because the program within our human consciousness does not reveal the illusion, but continues to carry on the illusion through language. Taking your life back is even being conscious of your language so that you will speak clearly and the words will not cover the way that you see yourself. When words are spoken that do not confirm the reality of love, they are an illusion.

The problem with humans is that most of what we fail to understand is that we are dreaming. This is because most of us have lost the five ways of the wise. We find ourselves caught up in other people's dramas and telling their stories within them. This gives us a source of life, but only for the moment. When you can believe there is something other than yourself, you can tune into the five ways of the wise. Life itself is the universe dreaming. The dream of the planet has the way of life. What you can discern as your own soul can be made up of dreams as well. There is nothing wrong with you trying yourself on many times. When you try on yourself for the first time, you may get put off, but you have to try on yourself with the idea that it is real. You can do this by saying, "This is myself and it is worth something." This way, the other voices in your head will go away. They will not have any power to even shout your identity. This is the confusion of most people. They think they are not worth anything, when they are alive in God. This is the truth of the alchemist. When you examine yourself again, you can hear the repetitive voices of all people building upon the illusion. These voices will be shut out when you know the truth. You can't stop the inner mind chatter without having anything to do with the five ways of the wise. Yet the five ways of the wise are in the dream itself. The dream itself contains the truth of all things, and the truth is projected as appearances until the projections fall away. Knowledge is the most powerful thing that you can attain. Love yourself deeply for greater results.

Through the ways of the wise, we are confronted with the power of self-consciousness. And this brought us to the point of a never-ending story, for in it we found the truth of the whole society, and of all humankind. The heartbeat of society pulses to stereotypical pattern of human emotion. It was a truth that was implanted in our soul so that we could awaken and know that the five ways of the wise are real. It gives us the power to know how to turn off the dream. Carl Jung said, "Your vision will become clear when you look inside your heart. Who looks outside, dreams. Who looks inside, awakens." So, look within.

Confronting the power of the illusion takes *concentration*. It takes concentration to hold onto an object, and it starts with being attentive to your own Being. Concentration is the ability we have to focus on an object of awareness. We can concentrate very deeply by using our attention. When we concentrate, we can place the object of awareness even inside our focus. By concentrating we learned the whole way of the wise and learned to discriminate our reality from the dreamworld.

We can attain self-mastery through concentration. As Buddha says in A Precious Garland verse 437, "Concentration is unafflicted one-pointedness."

When we are little children, we are taught to concentrate on certain ways that met our social roles, but often we lacked values and therefore, we did not express who we really are. Putting your life together requires at the minimum a value system. You automatically concentrated on what the teacher was teaching you, without thinking about it. Her values were your values. It is the same with our family values, and our religious values. We were taught to value our values with concentration, so they became the reason for our livelihood and what defined our self-identity. Without concentration, our values would diminish. Since the self became identified with these values, our Being would also diminish without concentration. When we begin to concentrate on our true values, we can find the old programs within human consciousness diminish. Thinking differently is what concentration requires. As we grow older, values are key to defining our identity. Values are the affirmations of what is real. Hold onto each one and they will be the support for you. Here the effort does not go unnoticed. Believe and you will succeed.

We are never taught to concentrate on our heart's desires. The outside world battles for the heart when we are children, and we gradually move away from the heart as we grow older because we place concentration on the wrong values and forget to value our heart values. This causes us needless suffering when we lose sight of the reason why we are here. We need to concentrate on what's important. If you could place your concentration on truth, you could awaken to the power within because truth holds the key to universal happiness, peace, and love. It takes concentration to value the values associated with truth, such as genuineness, authenticity, intuition, freedom, and happiness.

As children, we didn't have the opportunity to choose what to concentrate on. It was part of the program of our education, our upbringing, and our religion. The values that you concentrated on in these programs were unconscious and they were lived by automatically. We believed automatically everything we learned in these programs, and they started the powers of our mental concentration. This means we did not truly value our true values. The power of concentration creates a whole reality. The outside world starts the mind in concentration, and we are attentive to everything we see in the dream-world, instead of attentive to truth, but if we pay attention to our inner values, we can escape the power of the dream-world. Look no further; your true self is on the horizon.

Soul is what you will realize. The life that you have chosen in the five ways of the wise has this magical way to it because it is destined to be part of the chosen path. You're walking a certain way to live your dreams. For Taoism, The way was called ultimate reality. The doctrines of sacred scripture are the way itself. The life that you plan to lead always has something sacred in it. You can affirm your truth at any time. Being here is the cause of your celebration.

The five ways of the wise are the ways to realize Being. These ways of the wise can be discerned in the solving of life's greatest questions.

Let's start by asking, what is God? God is our peace. Whenever we feel ourselves letting go of the illusion, a sense of inner space is revealed and this, too, is God. He is the spaciousness of the eternal that invites us to share in the space free from the forms of consciousness and free from the prison. Abiding in this space is inner peace. There is space all around us that God reveals in the stillness of peace, and deep within you, you can feel the space each time in the air you breathe, and this is what awakens the heart of the peacemaker, who is not of this world, but of the heavenly kind, and his heart is the heart of God.

See the truth. There is a higher power.

Programming contains all of life's rules, laws, agreements, and commands, and they imprint patterns into the human consciousness that shapes our way of life. I call this process *the patterning of humankind*. In human patterning, the outside world imprints unto the inside world, and our original form becomes covered up through the superimposition of rules, codes, agreements, laws, and commands that are not focused on an all-embracing truth, but have their truth in the reality of denial. They are called *ego patterns*. The way itself is thought to be about all the patterns we receive, but with awareness we see these five ways of the wise at the core of our search for truth and meaning. Human patterning teaches us the ways to be in the outside world. The five ways of the wise teach you how to be yourself in the world within.

In becoming true to ourselves, we often find the striving of humankind to be made wise, yet the ego patterns stop us from aspiring to wisdom. These primarily include complaining, fighting against others and ourselves, and striving to be right. They give us the superimposition of the life that we call the ego. The ego projects a world within that is false. Through it, we perceive all things, but the world does not see us clearly; so the veil of illusion has to be lifted. Through human patterning we acquire the ways that we live by today from the cognitive unconscious, which continues to point us in the direction of the ways we learned as we were growing up. For example, in the face of confidence, a person may hold a negative belief pattern and state, "I'm not enough," instead of holding the positive belief pattern, "I'm enough." The negative belief creates a pattern that I have to do better. A sense of failure accompanies this belief, while the positive belief releases the patterns of inadequacy, incompetence, and imperfection. One can often find these ego patterns to be like stereotypes. Sometimes in our lives we can be part of a stereotype, but this is essentially what programs our minds when we grow older. The five ways of the wise will release this hold of stereotypes. They are five simple ways that challenge all the ways you learned before through human patterning. The secret endeavor is to lighten your life. Your journey continues by lifting the veil.

Life was here in your story as you were taught as a child. In human patterning, the voices we heard while we were growing up often imprinted our souls and shaped our behavior to the effect of patterning our minds away from truth, and away from the heart. This is because most of what we heard while growing up was part of the old program of human consciousness. Human patterning caused a separation from the heart and the mind. When there was separation, it caused the mind to think of another self. This was the entity known as the ego. It has to be seen for itself, in the light. The places where our minds create the separation is where we also create the suffering. If we do not follow the ways of the wise in our lifetime, the patterns will continue to shape our identities and they will form the basis for our false beliefs so that we grow up without ever encountering a vision as the alchemist had.

There is evidence of human patterning in ancient wisdom. It was a great concern for Plato in his *Republic*. He realized that children are patterned by the outside world with falsities, delusions, and lies, and he attempted to put in place a system of education to correct the human patterning. Plato described human patterning as a kind of soul-shaping. He realized that a child's soul is most malleable, like wax, and "it will take on any patterns one wishes to impress on it."[6] In a child's soul, there are not a lot of structures. They just radiate pure love. All their beliefs are not yet formed. Their minds need to be protected, and their hearts, because they have the truth

---

[6] *Republic* 377a11-b1, trans. By F. M. Cornford, in The Collected Dialogues of Plato, Ed. By Edith Hamilton and Huntington Cairns, Princeton: Princeton University Press

that we can be still real. Yet because of human patterning, the stories that children hear will corrupt their souls because, for the most part, it is opposite to what they will think when they are grown up. Human patterning does not operate with the truth in mind. In effect, when we are patterned as children, we often receive false beliefs that do not conform to an all-encompassing truth. The most predominant false belief comes from the fear that we are not loveable. What was once considered the Great Spirit is still alive when we consider that the trials and tribulations are making it seem to fall upon deaf ears.

Opinions are the most devastating in the system of human patterning. This is because children absorb opinions, and they are hard to erase, and they are likely to become unalterable. Those opinions rule our lives. In the ego patterns, we distort all those truths according to the opinions of all people. So, life is nothing but a distortion of the truth. We must be careful what we show to our children, for each story shapes his or her soul even more than a mother's handling and can imprint the soul with falsities. The power of human patterning sends ignorance into the human mind. It teaches children not to think for themselves. When we are set free in the system of mastery, we will find that we will regain these mental powers so that the human patterning can be corrected.

But what are we set free from? We are set free from the ego limitations and constraints that give us a crisis in identity. The fundamental problem of human patterning is that is creates self-ignorance. So, the solution is self-knowledge. This is where you can begin calculating what is right and wrong so that you can discern the truth within your own mind.

Turn your life over to the higher power.

All our conscious awareness is lost in the patterning of humankind. The patterning is so strong that we start to say and do things automatically, without thinking about it. The cognitive unconscious, in effect, is controlling our lives. Rather than making a conscious decision, we act unconsciously from habits from our program. All these patterns form the human consciousness that even overrides our free will, judgements, and rational decisions because the patterns act like laws, rules, and commands that we must follow in order to escape punishment and feel good. By valuing true values, you can begin to dissolve the human patterning. For a conscious acceptance of the new program, there has to be conscious acceptance of true values. These values are the basis of truth.

One can find transcendence when one takes the path of love. Transcendence will touch the heart of humankind ever more slightly with Christ.

Human patterning is behavioral training through reward and punishment. If the child does something right, the child gets a reward. If the child does something wrong, the child gets punished. This is what the educational system is supposed to correct, but in effect, it places more patterns into the soul so that life is lived by automatically. This causes the heart to be forgotten. Because the reward feels good, we form habits from the reward and go through life without valuing true values, but only following habits. We must break our habits associated with human patterning. We have to ask ourselves, "If it feels good, is it good?" The moral value associated with human patterning is lost because it creates ignorance, rather than knowledge. We have to awaken, but this can only come from breaking the patterns that programmed us. In the situation of the ego patterns, there is a battle, but this is also part of the pattern. This needs to be broken, like all the other ego patterns. So, the path of mastery will help you break these patterns so that you can see yourself clearly, as the way the teacher sees you. Your way of identifying your life is clearly identified with these ego patterns. You must drop the patterns completely or live a life of denial. You can be set free.

Sometimes the true self remains hidden within, and the old habits, ways, thoughts, and words have to be removed for the true self to be seen. You can't just order the true self to come into Being. There is a long start-to-finish process. That means you don't go on, without experiencing self-development. That is the perpetual nature of life. With one movement, it becomes an outward expression of the truth. Motion is taking you through the sands of time. There can be no moving forward without courage. It's the soul-force of the entity called life. It literally picks up the wounds and makes a start. It allows openness to penetrate into the soul so there can be deep healing. Without courage, there wouldn't be that love to move into the truth. Work is essential for your soul to be healed.

To awaken to truth, we must break our concentration with the old habits of each program in the systems we grew up with and choose consciously to value the values of the heart. Because it has to do with power, we must consciously choose to take our power back from all the areas that hold our attention. This includes breaking our habits, which are the cause of most of our suffering, and ending our false beliefs, which are predominantly linked to valuing values that are not heart-based. The result is to surrender to the heart and value new values of belonging and acceptance. What comes from valuing new values? *A new program. A new dream. A new you.* In the new era of wisdom, we can aspire to needing nothing, for it is in the reality of the coming of Christ. It is an emergent new consciousness. You will find a new way of Being. Look no further; your way is coming from God.

This is a new program for Heaven on Earth and a new life. With the dream of Heaven on Earth a reality, this will awaken your consciousness for planetary healing. It will create self-development that will allow you to achieve your dreams with power and a sense of adventure. Selfishness is the greatest of all these patterns that you will dissolve because you will drop your false self in the cause to love, give, and care for others. Your way to go through life will be altered considerably. The way that you think of things will be for love and the way that you move through life will be closer to the river that flows. In essence, you will feel that you can be a radiance of love and light. The hopes and dreams that you had can be fulfilled. This means that your soul can be revealed as God's own. You will show the world that you are a follower of love and light. Wisdom is the gift that you will receive from these five ways. Your heart can be healed. The motion of the river is true.

The new program is expressed in this parable in Buddhism. It goes like this:

"But to wear out your brain trying to make things into one without realizing that they are all the same — this is called 'Three in the morning'. What do I mean by 'three in the morning'? When the monkey trainer was handing out acorns, he said, 'You get three in the morning and four at night.' This made all the monkeys furious. 'Well, then,' he said, 'You get four in the morning and three at night.' The monkeys were all delighted. There was no change in the reality behind the words, and yet the monkeys responded with joy and anger. Let them, if they want to. So, the sage harmonizes both right and wrong and rests in Heaven the Equalizer. This is called walking two roads."[7] Love is reality that you can create with your word.

In the new program, you will find the happiness that the monkey trainer knew was possible even for the monkeys. It was not too late for the monkeys to see that they had a truth as well. Your road of self-development is made possible in the new program. This makes your healing possible. The parable teaches that the reality does not change, although the program changes with the words. As Buddha says in the Lankavatara Sutra verse 61, there is an eternal abiding reality where the substance of truth abides forever. So, this is a paradox, yet it is so profound that we realize that the power of words can harmonize our reality or create pain. When you see that

---

[7] 365 Spirit: A Daily Journey For Your Soul, by Aaron Zerah, Writings of Chuang-Tzu.

reality can be shifted with language, you will see how the five ways of the wise can shift your reality to truth. The word is the seed. It is no wonder this place discovered is called Heaven, for the life that the monkey trainer tried to create was pure and good by comparing the two realities and by walking the two roads. Life can tell you that there is a true self that is made possible by knowing the great wisdom.

The life that you want from the new program doesn't follow anything but the way of Heaven. Here, you can find your Being whole and complete.

We have a tendency to forget what we really are. We forget our authenticity. It is essential to affirm your truth over and over again to unlearn the ego's patterns. This is so that we learn the new program. Your thoughts can become things.

There is a life that you can attain from this new language. And here you can learn to speak impeccably so that your language causes happiness. It will show you that you are present in your Being for an eternity. When we hear about language being damaging to our minds and bodies, we say this is Hell. We have created a way out of Hell with the five ways of the wise. The way the monkey trainer attempted to love was perfect. He removed the old program and replaced it with a new program simply by speaking impeccably.

The sadness of most people is that they do not see that the two roads are comparable in their lives. When we continue to use language that is destructive, we cause death, and when our language reflects love, we create life. In Psalm 1:6, the Lord declared that there are two ways of reality like these two roads: "For the LORD watches over the way of the righteous, but the way of the wicked leads to destruction." In Jeremiah 21:8, it says, "Furthermore, tell the people, 'This is what the LORD says: See, I am setting before you the way of life and the way of death.'" We have to be conscious that there are two roads there for us at all times that are made evident in the way we speak, and choose to walk the way of life and the way of the virtuous mind, speaking impeccably. You will unlearn the old program when you replace your old language with a new language. This will create a transformation in your consciousness. Make an effort to reflect the truth of your Being in your language. The construction of your reality depends upon your power to speak in the light, thereby destroying the darkness. Life is the reflection of love.

In the core of your creation, there is a blueprint that can materialize your way of existence. It is not disguised in the ego patterns. Knowing the truth of who you are is built into the blueprint. Knowing that you can be authentic is restarting the original blueprint and shattering the old program. Therefore, the ways of the wise are helpful for this restart. The lostness that you sense without Christ can be lifted in the practice so that the Kingship in our heredity will be sealed. The power of human emotion lies in the detriment that humankind will not feel safe.

The direction that you want to go is Heaven-bound. Human patterning does not teach us the truth of life's greatest questions. In fact, it instils programs, rather than questioning. It does not teach us how to be a philosopher.

The alchemist learns the truth when he hears it from his inner guru. He is set free and attained enlightenment, which shifted his space of awareness away from the ego, which is imprinted by patterns of falsity, to his true self, which is eternal, immortal and divine. Truth is the eye and it should be made to say something alive in the space of awareness. By understanding the knowledge of sacred wisdom, the knowledge has the power to set the alchemist free from human patterning. Your wholeness is predicated on wisdom.

Most people have identified with their false self all their lives. They do not believe in their eternality, their immortality, or their divinity. They hear that they are imperfect most of their lives and identify with this self-image. The patterns of imperfection, emptiness, and incompleteness form their self-image. The standard of life today makes the Universal Ugly comparable to the homelessness of a wealthy person. That is what the outside world wants us to identify with, with the images of the self, which are all created by the patterning of humankind. We are patterned by images, not by truth. So we begin living a life based on opinions, not based on truth. The revelation of the true self gives you a new self to identify with in your Being. Being born again is the birth of wisdom. Life can come from this true self.

You can compare this new self, the true self, to the false self. Realize that where the false self is limited and has death built right in, the true self, by virtue of being without conditions, being pure love, is limitless. In essence, you are given a new self, one of pure, unconditional love. This stops the imprints on your soul from human patterning, and all the images of imperfection are dropped. You can stop judging yourself against a false image and stop holding false beliefs about yourself when you listen to the truth about the self. To disbelieve this truth is to deny our original form. While growing up, we did not have the awareness of what we were until it is transferred by way of patterning into our original formless purity. The truth was then hidden from us. What was hidden can be found.

But we have to back up, and rewind to undo the fundamental untruth that has been patterned onto our soul. The old program categorizes our thoughts, beliefs, feelings, and ways of Being. It is as if the world never existed without light. What can be worse that the knowledge of darkness? The untruth categorizes yourself as unnecessary and unwanted and it is reinforced by a set of false beliefs. He who holds the truth can shine as if a mirror into the sight of blind eyes so they will see through the darkness that what was one story can be lived as reality.

He or she who wants to have truth revealed must endeavor to ask the right questions, like, "Where did it all begin?" and "Why am I here?" These two questions can birth a philosophy of self-consciousness. Simply inquiring within can open the doors of the human mind. Human patterning is where the philosophy of self-consciousness is denied because it does not allow your Being to grow through questioning. Perhaps the most powerful way of human patterning is through social rules, ethical codes of conduct, norms, morals, and standards of morality. The five ways of the wise can be considered rules of life. "Don't say mean things to other people" is one code of conduct; another is "Talk to each other politely"; another is to "wash yourself clean", and by far the most desired is "God, be with me when I die." To know what a code is in the mind of your family is one thing, but to know what it is in the mind of yourself is another, for there are rules that can be enlivened by the study of sacred texts in your own Being. These have to do with a fundamental way of transformation. You can change your beliefs and your mind if you think that your programming gives you rules that have come from an era of greatness. Other rules that include personal transformation include, "Walk with your head out of the crowd", "Don't listen to fools", "Keep an eye on the prize", and "To each his own". Social rules and ethical codes are never so connected to family as when you are growing up; so, you can undo the human patterning when you study the ways of the wise and reprogram yourself with ways that are based on all-encompassing truth. This way has to do with the peace that can be attained through knowledge of the world in a peaceful state. It is not that we are recreating the peaceful state in our mind's eye, but that we are welcoming "what is" to come into being and fruition, and this can only come from knowledge. May the truth impart wisdom to you.

The knowledge that I have outlined here has to do with the greatness of sacred wisdom found in world religions. The five ways of the wise contain five essential teachings spoken about in world religion. Religions have attempted to come into conformity with each other on these topics. The religions that we find are in the same

54

meaning bracket. The eight major world religions are Christianity, Confucianism, Buddhism, Hinduism, Islam, Judaism, Taoism, and Zoroastrianism. They were created in a profound manner, by the greatest of prophets and people on the planet. He or she who enquires into the world order will be accounted for in the ordered existence that the Masters of life call the way. The way cannot be told to all people, but all people have access to knowing the Way. Light is often thought of as the way. It is courage that takes you there. There is peace of heart in this knowledge. May you accept the wisdom as truth.

But these teachings are often lost by the countless patterns that have come into society that sought to program our ways of life, our family, our educational systems, and our Being according to an illusion. The result is that the oneness of world religions has been covered up. Knowledge of the five ways of the wise can lead to a better life. When one wonders about how these world religions have attempted to agree on these five topics, this takes hold of the issue of human patterning and starts the new program of truth.

Wondering about the five ways of the wise immediately brings you to a way of reduction that it is all physical, when in fact, the truth is that there is a mental phenomenon that is taking place. This mental phenomenon is the essence of John Godfrey Saxe's parable of the Blind Men and The Elephant. This famous Indian fable tells the story of six blind travelers that come across different parts of an elephant in their life journeys. In each instance, each blind man creates his own version of truth and reality from the subjective and limited perspective. It goes like this:

It was six men of Indostan,
To learning much inclined,
Who went to see the Elephant
(Though all of them were blind),
That each by observation
Might satisfy his mind.

The First approach'd the Elephant,
And happening to fall
Against his broad and sturdy side,
At once began to bawl:
"God bless me! But the Elephant
Is very like a wall!"

The Second, feeling of the tusk,
Cried, "Ho! what have we here
So very round and smooth and sharp?
To me 'tis mighty clear,
This wonder of an Elephant
Is very like a spear!"

The Third approach'd the animal,
And happening to take
The squirming trunk within his hands,
Thus boldly up and spake:
"I see," — quoth he — "the Elephant
Is very like a snake!"

The Fourth reached out an eager hand,

And felt about the knee:
"What most this wondrous beast is like
Is mighty plain," — quoth he —
"'Tis clear enough the Elephant
Is very like a tree!"
The Fifth, who chanced to touch the ear,
Said — "E'en the blindest man
Can tell what this resembles most;
Deny the fact who can,
This marvel of an Elephant
Is very like a fan!"
The Sixth no sooner had begun
About the beast to grope,
Then, seizing on the swinging tail
That fell within his scope,
"I see," — quoth he, — "the Elephant
Is very like a rope!"

And so these men of Indostan
Disputed loud and long,
Each in his own opinion
Exceeding stiff and strong,
Though each was partly in the right,
And all were in the wrong!
MORAL,

So, oft in theologic wars
The disputants, I ween,
Rail on in utter ignorance

Of what each other mean; And prate about an Elephant not one of them has seen!"[8]

The parable teaches you that truth is relative to each person's perspective, and if each person represented a world religion, they would be competing with each other over their version of reality. The parable denies that there can be only one truth, but shows that there are many acceptable truths, given that the blind men cannot see with eyes of truth. The simple truth this teaches is that our life experiences limit our sensory perceptions and our knowledge, so objective truth is not possible. For many people, this goes against their moral intuition. People can easily come up with moral claims that seem universal. For example, 1. Do not kill innocent people. 2. Do not cause unnecessary pain or suffering. 3. Do not lie or deceive. 4. Do not steal or cheat. 5. Keep your promises and honor your contracts. 6. Do not deprive another person of his or her freedom. 7. Do justice, treating people as they deserve to be treated. 8. Help other people, especially when the cost is minimal. These ethical rules are even programmed into us through human patterning. What these principles all have in common is that they contribute to human flourishing in society. This is the essence of a healthy society. In other words, a society without these moral principles will not function for very long. It would be ideal if all ego patterns of thought could reflect the intention of happiness, truth, goodness, and beauty, but instead, they program an illusion of the self

---

[8] The Blind Men and The Elephant, Mastering Project Work, By David M. Schmaltz

as limited, imperfect, and incomplete, and sustain the outside dream.

A judgement is subjective if true and false statements arise because of what we think. A judgement is objective regardless of anyone's thoughts on the matter. It is true that one person with a limited perception of truth cannot say this is the way of all reality or of truth. The parable teaches you that one person's access to reality is not the same for the others, so there are different versions of truth, or many ways of reality that can be known. This is a positive of moral relativism. The five ways of the wise reveal that there are moral principles that apply to everyone, and these moral ideas are not just opinions and preferences of individuals or cultures, but very real instances of objective, even universal truth. The theories of moral objectivism and ethical relativism each represent different answers to the question, "What is truth?" A truth is the revelation of a universal occurrence in creation. What is universal is for all humankind, by virtue of true humanity. Ethical Relativism holds the thesis that there are no objective, universal moral principles that are valid for all people. In short, ethical relativists believe that moral ideas are a matter of societal norms or personal opinion, and are therefore not binding upon others. The ethical relativist promotes that these versions of truth should be tolerated. That's what makes ethical relativism attractive. But clearly, there are some practices that should not be tolerated. There are common ideas like, "Who's to say who is right?" and "What's right for one person may not be right for another," and "Who am I to judge?" However, this theory cannot support a principle of universal tolerance because the ethical relativist cannot support any universal principle. The ethical relativist will look at the differences of opinion among people and cultures regarding how to approach ethics, including how to identify objective moral principles, and make the conclusion that because there is diversity, and even uncertainty, among moral views, and differing moral situations, there is no objective right and wrong. The parable is often argued to promote tolerance and diversity. The statement, "What is right for you may not be right for me" is an example of ethical relativism, more specifically ethical subjectivism, which holds that all moral principles are justified only by the individual, and do not necessarily apply to people other than the individual who accepts them. While ethical relativism is popular and many people are drawn to it is as a means to avoid having their views examined and criticized by others, the reality is that it simply is not a functional ethical theory that works in the real world.

The West has been exposed to the ancient Greek philosopher Protagoras (450 BCE), who was a moral relativist. He defined knowledge as that which is derived from one person's tastes and said that we make our own truth. Protagoras said, "Man is the measure of all things: of those that are, that they are, of those that are not, that they are not."[9] He is describing how the human is first and foremost measure of himself, with all his qualities,

---

[9] *Theaetetus* 71a. trans. By F. M. Cornford, in The Collected Dialogues of Plato, Ed. Edith Hamilton and Huntington Cairns, Princeton: Princeton University Press.

characteristics, abilities, and desires. Plato wrote against Protagoras because he believed the thesis was logically incoherent. Plato says, "Protagoras, admitting as he does that everyone's opinion is true, must acknowledge the truth of his opponent's belief about his own belief, where they think he is wrong."[10] Plato's argument is a form of a *reductio ad absurdum* argument. This kind of argument proves relativism is false because it leads to an "absurdity". This implies there is a contradiction. To do the *reductio* proof, we have to first assume the opposite of what we want to prove. We then assume the argument is false, but reducing it to absurdity. Having derived a contradiction, we prove that relativism is false. Relativism preaches that there is not some objective reality that is the same for all people. It is the denial of ethical universalism. It says that reality is particular to only one person at any given moment. The significance of one's perceptions changes from moment to moment according to one's own tastes. In sum, relativism is the view that truth itself and the values inherent in a truth statement vary from context to context and person to person.

Life really involves the practice of knowing what is good and what is bad.

In this parable, there is a concrete area of reality which is much more difficult to ignore, and there is a grey area which is not concrete. Understanding what the concrete area is, is the power of love. You can always

---

[10] Ibid., p. 876.

attend to this concrete area with knowledge of the way things are. It is difficult, if not impossible, to get at a thing completely, but this does not mean that we cannot get at it "enough" to consider it a truth and therefore reality. It is not just about having enough to agree upon as evidence to say it is the way a thing is, because clearly not all evidence is equal. So, acquiring evidence for some things can be extremely difficult, like acquiring evidence for the existence of the atom prior to our modern technology. But the evidence we can acquire can lead to knowledge of truth itself. And we can discern what the ways of the wise are from this knowledge where all religions have attempted to agree upon the truth statements. In this case, none are blind men, but all have access to discourse, and this leads to agreement and universalism. The parable shows that we recognize reality from the knowledge we have of other things, making all perception to be conditioned by previous experiences. But this clearly shows there is a God's eye point of view, although none of the people can see this view because they are blind.

Surely, then, there is something bigger than this on the horizon. The parable shows that total reality is more, and much more that the expansion of its parts. It is not a question of relativism, and the truth of all religions, but of believing that there is one higher truth that can never be attained by our partial truths. The fact that many people don't know what reality is does not mean that objective reality does not exist. In fact, it can mean just the opposite, that the blind men are trying to access a totality that exists for all people to discover, and that totality points to something bigger indeed — *namely, the elephant.*

In the Chinese Tao, it is said that reality is a totality of complementary principles. When speaking on how the male and female yin and yang are in one another, Joseph Campbell said, "The dark has a light spot and the light has a dark spot — that's how they can relate to one another."[11] There is a pursuit of intelligence to understand the five ways of the wise, so that we can understand why truth claims are not just relative. The result of such intelligence is the way we move into society faster than we did in the past, because this shows that this way is not subordinate to the path of life. We can escape from the narrative of being dead. This is a great escape.

Sometimes the life that we are leading is not so clear; so we can see many points of relativity. We can turn our life into casting a story that shows us the way of our minds in the drama. Then we can get lost again until we are reminded again about the parable of the Blind Men and the Elephant; so we can't deny that there is something like the elephant. It is the way of the lost to fill themselves up, but we know this is a product of their stereotypical belief pertaining to a false identity. Yet we can't deny that we tend to see what we want to see, what we are "looking for". The ways of the elephant show at least six ways of reality in this situation; so there are greater things that can come from one perspective. But he who knows the cosmos knows there are five ways of the

---

[11] Joseph Campbell and the Power of Myth - TV.

wise. The cosmos was a construction, not a mind. It was placed within the reality that God created. He created the cosmos knowing there would be something perfect in it, because he was perfect. You will be truly awakened when you understand the perfection is also in you. You can know this reality and participate in it with devotion to truth. When you imagine you are there with God, it becomes real when you accept the truth; that you are there with God. Just as you continue your journey, take note of how the way can be revealed.

The parable not only points to physical blindness, but points to spiritual blindness as well. This points us in the direction that our eyes need to be opened to see the truth so that we can directly experience the totality. Surely, we are all blind to some degree. While it's true that we all have a limited scope of perception at times, our eyes can be opened through discourse. What they were seeking is an answer to the question, "What were they being made to discover?" It can only be a matter of spirit when we consider these people to be from different world religions. This shows that there is not equality, but world perplexity. Coming into the oneness that we seek to attain is about turning to the light. The light produces salvation for all people. The light will uncover the darkness through discourse. Knowing that there can be a discourse is what can bring salvation as well. Spiritual ignorance is what the darkness refers to. There can be no cause for ignorance in that place with the elephant if there is discourse. Discourse is of solving the basic question.

What is the light, but the five ways of the wise? When you come upon the light, you can be sure it will release the stereotypes that the parable of the elephant showed. Love is not possible in moral relativism. So, we have to aim higher than this theory. The cosmic awareness of the elephant is within all people so that they can be tuned into their knowledge of what life is so that they won't be left out in the cold. The light that we have within us will not be taken from us and with it, you will recover your sanity from the illnesses that were in the mind. When you talk with wisdom, you can clean up the sadness that is part of the needless suffering from these illnesses. Then you will attain freedom from the revelation of truth. What has been discovered is that your past is unacceptable to your self-transformation and needs to be let go because it only serves to contribute more pain and suffering. Love will not be lost in the transformation from one thing to the next.

When you consider that the foundation of yourself can be set with these five ways of the wise, you can find hope, and this is cause for transforming your life even for a higher good. These five ways of the wise are the new program of humankind. They will, in effect, release you from the hold of any previous programs. When we consider the global awakening that we are part of, it is undeniable that it involves the five ways of the wise. Use them to support a new way of Being.

The "something" that is troubling you cannot be solved with the elephant parable. It must be solved with a glimpse of the elephant itself. This involves grasping that the totality involves not just masculine and feminine principles, but an eternal soul that can be called your own. So, the five ways of the wise involves giving you the space of infinity, where before the false beliefs declared you a limited being. So that what you long for, you can behold. Nothing can take away the five ways of the wise from the one who can see the whole. It is as if they are privileged in the beginning to come upon the Mind of God. The five ways of the wise are not just spiritual evolution, but they are a truth that defies mediocrity. This truth that is known to the one person that sees the whole is like cosmic consciousness. The perspective of the cosmic man is godlike. He can turn his mind not to just being "here", but to places that are in the beyond. This consciousness that he has is not just vast, but is to be thought of as the beyond. When one can perceive his likeness in all things, then he is cosmically aware. So, you have the opportunity to ask yourself the right questions. This gives you the truth of love. One can turn this love, which is an emotion, into a fact of one's mind. Something that tells you that you are cosmically aware is called the way. So, you should be turning your life into becoming like God. There is never any doubt that you can find the way when you have cosmic awareness. Your soul is not lost when you have found the way of transformation. Your life will be molded away from the human patterning to something that is eternal light. This will make the transformation of letting these past patterns go easier, for they are holding you back from knowing the truth. The knowledge that you have gained already is part of the process of truth. Here leadership involves a tremendous effort.

Here we have set out the purpose of your transformation. What is transformation, but the way of light? This makes it hard to forget that there were decades of horror-filled social orders that renounced or shied away from the truth being revealed here. The root question is, "What can we do to accommodate our fears?", since our past traumas and suffering are what is causing the disbelief in peace on earth to begin with. It is only by living more freely; then we can be set free ourselves. Simply by looking at the way of the world, we can see that world peace is a practical solution to all of life's problems. It takes very little effort to read through these five ways of the wise to awaken to a better reality. The world needs more wisdom. What was once lost a long time ago can be recovered. The soul has a remarkable way of mending itself. The program of peace is what we want to recover, for this will set us free. The way to recover this peace is by reaffirming that life has value. The soul-transforming way of the philosopher is not to be abandoned. It is the gift of all humankind to find the gold within. If you think that you have lost your way, just attune yourself to the philosopher's way. It can be found by rewinding the program.

Everything that you think can be real is already real in the mind of God. Let us rewind back to a time of ancient civilization when countless codes were introduced into humankind by the seers and the way-showers. Most of these codes became universalized, but five of them remained true even for the family. Human patterning can be the opposite of life. We will look to the divinity found in the sacred texts and through our admiration for their order, goodness and perfection; we will start on the path of transforming our soul from what the human patterning created, to the vision that the alchemist revealed in his messages.

Enrich your spirit.

Human patterning came down to us through generations of evil and filled our lives with terror, and it was only the way of the philosopher that could find the proper ways of truth that could save his soul. Evil came into the world because the self-consciousness would not allow the light to shine. Mental patterning is what each facet of the human psyche contains. It is not just good enough to ask, "Are we programmed?", but we have to ask, "What patterns have imprinted our souls?" and "What programs are running our lives?" There are the past programs for living, for raising family, for education, for society, for political order, for religion, for work, for relationships, and for ourselves. But the most powerful programs are those that we have for ourselves. There is even a world program. What the programs involve is a categorization of the human mind into a limited and dependent existence. You will attain a great life from attaining the sacred wisdom.

If we imagine our minds as a great computer that is created by a Designer, then it may seem obvious that we are running on a deliberative sequence preconceived by the Designer and even encoded in our very DNA by programs to attain a destined choice by a certain means. Free will is absent from the equation, since all that we do is go from program to program, and live according to patterns, without coming to any deliberate conclusion. The idea that the world's a stage and we are merely actors upon the stage or puppets in a play carrying out the purposeful will of the Director comes to mind. In order for us to have creative input in the decision-making and thereby find our free will, we must deprogram ourselves from the roles and masks that make life without conscious causation. The roles that we take on are job, relationship, religion, education, parenthood, protector and provider. These roles are often very fixed, and we start holding a belief-set pertaining to our roles that defines our identity, yet we have a crisis of identity when we lack truth. This is a distortion in the way people perceive themselves. For example, in the mind's eye, you feel one thing about yourself, but in the egoic mind, you say another. This means that you have to say what you feel, because the feeling is the essence of your Being. We create all sorts of suffering when we fail to meet our roles and do not live up to their expectations. So, look within.

Although there may be many deliberative paths on the journey that are compatible with any number of choices, they will only feel like "me" or "mine" when I break free from the programming, stop the world patterns and conform to the heavenly ones set down for me by sacred wisdom. Sacred wisdom allows us to regain conscious power to make deliberative choices and cause our own destinies to unfold. At the onset of our ability to need programs was terror. This took human beings away from the light. It can be found again very simply by appealing to world religions and world scripture. This scripture gives us the fundamental truths of humankind. It is as if we have longed for this all our lives. What can be greater than knowledge of the truths of humankind that would give us the ability to recover our true selves and find peace? The world program would limit ourselves and insist that dark would overshadow the light, but this program would not sustain itself through the light of sacred wisdom.

But what makes these five ways of the wise stand out from the rest of the codes that were passed down to humankind? They are conducive to spreading the light, to you being the light. That is what truth essentially is: light.

The truth is not only revealed, but it is given so that the way can be manifested in your daily lives. What brings us to this point of manifestation is that there is a point to you being here. "Truly being here is glorious,"[12] says Rilke in the *Seventh Duino Elegy*. It cannot be taken away from you, that you are the light. There is a never-ending cause for your purpose to realize this truth. What has been found to be the darkness is really selfishness. Giving back is the way. What you don't realize is that this turn for your self-realization is global. It can't get any greater than this. Heaven on Earth is the profound wisdom that you seek. This is your soul attuning itself to the light. This is what it means to be more conscious. To begin with, it is about finding the truth within ourselves, instead of blindly allowing ourselves to be programmed, either from society, or from others, or even from our own inner voice, which can be inauthentic and disturb the truth of love. Your voice is inauthentic if it emphasizes that you are limited and incapable of becoming what God

---

[12] My Bright Abyss: Meditation of a Modern Believer, by Christian Wiman.

has in store for us, and your voice is authentic if it tells the truth of who you really are.

To get out of it, we have to accept the responsibility to deprogram our minds from all self-limiting beliefs that we have bought into that reinforce a false self, and reprogram our minds with the five ways of the wise so we can master life. He who has the power within can reprogram himself consciously. The life that you seek to attain is not without reach. Coming to grips with being "here", rather some other distant place, is what it takes. You can attain the realization that you are with God with the five ways of the wise. Knowledge is where truth is found. The price paid for the loss of consciousness was a darkening of humanity; so, turning to the light is the price that you need to pay to recover.

Think only of your truth when you try to reprogram your mind.

Looking back on your past issues, you will find that many times you have been deceived. What you thought was real was not only a delusion; it was a lie. This is termed waking up when you can see the light. Happiness starts here. The great wisdom also starts here. In the program of creation, there was a story that they used to tell you about the beginning of humankind. It was in this program that they used to tell you that there was a grievous error. Something went wrong in the story of creation. It was not time for the truth to come out. It would take centuries before the truth could be revealed. Having come to terms with the fact that there was a grievous error propels the search for revelation. It was ever more self-evident that this error could be the cause of darkness. Whether or not we can see the truth is up to us. Go back to the time before Noah's Ark. Your heredity is at stake. Gone are the days of trust and love. Too many fools have come onto the planet to say this time is not going forward. Revisiting this time of Noah's Ark, we can see that this was a time when plentitude came on the planet. Can this time ever be discovered again simply by believing in the five ways of the wise? This is the path of the wise man to say that it is possible because inherent in these ways is generation, and this is what is needed to start again. There was a downfall on planet Earth, and this is why we are left to feel forgotten. In the hopes of restoring our Earth, we can place our trust in vanquishing the state of depravity. So, we can go forward with the wise man. The Path has within itself the acceptance that you need to go forward. Accept the facts.

Where did it all start to turn around for Noah? It was in his identity with God that he could quiet the angers of the fields of viciousness and lift up the life-forms that he had been entrusted to, to start again. Noah was not a poor man in his heart. And it is this attunement to your heart that you will learn how to do in this revealing. He who learns to quiet the fields like Noah will find that there can be a fresh start. What was going on at that time long ago was not a deliverance into the hand of God, but it was a foreshadowing of the coming of new life. This is coming into reality with the truth that we have been given here. It is not a self-deprecating existence when there is the foreshadowing of new life. This is a wholesomeness produced in the era of love and light. God has declared and said that these times are here for renewing. The truth contained within world scripture is not easily understood, but with certainty, it can be known.

He or she who knows about the patterning of humankind can stop the programmer that is doing damage to even our cellular level in our minds and bodies. Once you learn one way of the wise, you will of necessity shake the ground that you are walking upon. When you have an epiphany about truth, it will give you self-confidence. The very ground that you thought was real will be upheaved when you come into truth. And this is your coming into Heaven. The propensity to shake this ground is cause for further dissolution from everything that is false. By shaking the ground, we may feel faint at first until we transcend even the illegality of what Hitler was doing. He knew how to program people into a self-consciousness that would take them away almost forever from the truths that were hiding in the fragments of world religions. We cannot forget what his voice was doing because it was there to end the self-consciousness of light. What moves us forward is not so much the notion of light, but the goal that we have in mind, to be the light. This gives us the power of transcendence and overcoming. It is never too far from our minds what the darkness contains.

What was human patterning when it was time to know God? This was a time when we could ask ourselves if there are ways to live by that could govern our lives and our conduct. This is the introduction of five ways of the wise. Ethical codes and rules make us fail at life or succeed. They are guidelines of political correctness that reinforce ethical conduct. These codes are written in a social system governed by power structures to guide behavior based on moral values. They lessen the burden of gray areas and define moral guidelines for conduct. There are thousands of codes that we live by, both consciously and unconsciously, that define our behavior. Chances are if you are failing at life, you have to change the rules you live by. This often requires that we change our thinking if the ways that we live by are making us suffer by living an inauthentic life.

By adapting to these five ways of the wise, you will become empowered to become a Master of life. If you want to transform your life and find happiness, you have to stop using the ways that patterned your false self with lies and start using the five ways of the wise to reprogram yourself with the truth. Only the truth will set you free. Happiness is the effect of wisdom. You have to find the courage to end your dependency on the ways that affirm a fear-based reality. When we fear, we lose energy and become depleted. One of these fear-based beliefs teaches us that we must live up to religious beliefs or we will go to Hell. There is really no reason to fear life when you have this set of ways as your personal power because they give you access to a higher structure of reality, of truth, of purpose, of goodness, and of power itself. They are, in fact, where personal power derives from.

Soul is your destiny.

What is power? Power is a faculty within our minds that gives us an ability to move. With the five ways, you can speak up and be in your power. They are the means to an end, and the end is love itself. They are purposive. They are meaningful because they allow us to achieve our goals and realize our dreams. You have come into an existence of power when you have found the truth. This is the way to live a flourishing life. It is the way to start your life anew. There is an eternal way in every way of power. It gives you the knowledge to know what is right and what is wrong. This will teach you a system of greatness. Power is the way of consciousness.

The five ways have the power to transform you.

The First Way of The Wise:
The Golden Rule

The first way of the wise is the Golden Rule. It states, "Do unto others as you would have them do unto you." The first way is the most important because you will have the ability to attain wisdom with this way alone and create Heaven on Earth. You can find within this rule the way of the Masters. It introduces an idea into your mind that will allow you to grasp the truth that the ancients knew was here, and that could be revealed to those that sought it out. It has the power of lifting the veils of ignorance and letting the light shine in so that people can transcend their everyday realities. The Golden Rule is an instance of moral objectivism, which holds that there are objective, universal truths called moral principles that are valid for all people. The first way of the wise sounds very simple, even self-evident. Doing something gives you the power of action, and this gives you the power of productivity. You can put this first truth into action. Then the reality of love will materialize even quicker. When you change your own world, other people will start changing around you. But you have to work on yourself. This will create a ripple in humanity, and the effort you put into your life will be transformed. The life activation that you seek is real.

The first way of the wise is to do unto others as you would have them do unto you. This is a very powerful way because it has been agreed upon by every major world religion, and by other religions including the Baha'i Faith, Jainism, Native Spirituality, Sikhism, and Unitarianism. For example, in Christianity in the book of Matthew, chapter 22, verses 36-40, it says, "'Teacher, which is the great commandment in the law?' Jesus said to him, "'You shall love the Lord your God with all your heart, and with all your soul, and with all your mind." This is the great and first commandment. And the second is like it, "You shall love your neighbor as yourself." On these two commandments depend all the law and the prophets.'" There was a way that Confucius wrote this rule as well in *Analects*, verse 12:2. He says, "Do unto another what you would have him do unto you, and do not unto another what you would not have him do unto you. Thou needest this law alone. It is the foundation for all the rest." In Buddhism in the Sutta Nipata, verse 705, Buddha says, "Comparing oneself to others in such terms as 'Just as I am, so are they, just as they are so am I', he should neither kill nor cause others to kill." In Native Spirituality, Chief Dan George says, "We are as much alive as we keep the earth alive."

What few people realize is that this rule was first stated by the philosopher Aristotle (385 BC), who says, "We should conduct ourselves toward others as we would have them act toward us."[13] All that has been revealed is the work of the prophets and the wise. We can attest to their being something true in each saying.

What is true is that there is an overarching love that came down from the heavens to bless the earth profoundly. The Golden Rule professes to an earthly kingdom, and it can be accessed by loving-kindness. For those that know the Golden Rule, they know something very profound. It is as if there is a ripple in the wave of consciousness, in the virtue of humanity. The ripple stirs the mind's eye in the deep recesses of the human heart. There can never be another space like this earth-shattering rule because it reveals there is something that transcends our humanity within all of us. You can find your life being made better simply by talking about the Golden Rule. This shows that the reality of life had an attunement to something greater.

The coming upon truths in the world is made evident through the way things are done in the world. This way is by rules and codes of conduct as they mirror the truth that a great thing can be manifested. The first way of the wise is a tool for transformation. Like all codes of conduct, it can be used to measure our history and teach us who came into being to show us the way. The most powerful rules become laws that instill and protect ways of life. He or she who goes through life without knowing a single rule is barely human. So, it can benefit immensely to know at least one rule of humankind. They

---

[13] Theosophical Siftings, Volume 5, p. 19.

will undo the false belief that has been programmed into our minds concerning the impending darkness of all people, and the inability to be the light. What has been attested to for thousands of years is that we can function to higher and higher means of productivity, and by so doing what is productive, we can spread the light, thereby increasing the frequency of our own planetary vibration, which is suffering with the darkness of false beliefs.

The first way of the wise is found in this first universal rule. Most people have heard of The Golden Rule. Here is the life that you want to have. The heart of transformation is the ability to love. We demonstrate this ability in the Golden Rule. It requires switching our places with the other person according to our principle of empathy and responding to each situation according to our ability to relate to the other person by being in their shoes. Are there rules for life? According to ethical universalism, we should conduct and govern ourselves according to the universal rules. In other words, we should live by a set of rules. We take turns in the Golden Rule to not be complacent. So, we have the purpose and the drive to overcome our selfishness. Heaven on Earth is life-changing wisdom because you will find an error-free society and an inbuilt strategy for keeping the world together. The Golden Rule gives us a heart for humankind. We can learn to serve the less fortunate, and be kind to one another in the process, as well as be responsible for our actions. Essentially, the Golden Rule is an act of loving-kindness that is motivated by self-love. When I imagine what it would be like to have something done to me in the same situation, I am guided by loving-kindness. By questioning how my action would affect the other person, I am guided by loving-kindness. This is the way of the Masters. If you feel that you are wrestling with God, know that your kindness can lead to His wisdom.

The future self is ready to be made responsible by following the Golden Rule.

You have within your own mind your soul to consider in each situation; so, this gives you a greatness within to hold onto your soul. Brilliant people have proclaimed the Golden Rule is the sole way to create a moral order and have affirmed the Golden Rule is the heart of morality. More cultures have adopted this principle as a way of life, so it is the most powerful way of the wise. In each case of assessing the Golden Rule in situations, you must take a test for consistency that establishes whether or not you are willing to do the same thing in a situation if this act was done to you. By understanding whether or not the action passes the test of consistency, you make the decision of what to do in that situation. This means that you can't go wrong. This implies that you will care about the other person as you would care about yourself. That is to say, you will see the other as an end in herself and not as a means to your own ends.

The Golden Rule can bring about peace. It transcends all individuality and cultural differentiation and simply puts forth a universal rule for all, without calling it the Buddhist Golden Rule, or the Christian Golden Rule, or the Hindu Golden Rule, and so forth. This ends the potential conflict among religions and unites them within a moral conviction. Indeed, this is why the Golden Rule makes an attempt at global peace. It will stabilize our society and improve the quality of one's life.

The Golden Rule encourages a mind of compassion. Although this virtue is difficult to attain, it is worthwhile to try to achieve with the first way of the wise. But what is compassion? True compassion stems from a deep bond with other human beings and creatures that makes the moral conviction that I am like other people and I do not want them to suffer seem intuitively right, because I know deep within my own truth that I do not want to suffer; so I want to help them overcome the causes of suffering and find true happiness. Any feeling of difference between oneself and others, such as resentment and ill-will, comes from a heart that lacks compassion, and these feelings will create a conflict with the other person. The heart of compassion is the heart of truth. It bears the responsibility that you have with all other creatures. This lifts you up to a place of equality with those creatures so that the Golden Rule can be implemented. The Golden Rule has truth-bearing within it because it can look at these other human beings and creatures and say they are not to be harmed. This is the essence of compassion. It is these efforts in the first way of the wise that will heal your hearts. When you are compassionate, you can stop judgement from happening. There will be less evil in the world.

The Golden Rule emphasizes personal responsibility. Take responsibility for your actions. When we are responsible, we are conscious of there being situations that can cause suffering to all people, and to animals and the whole planet. To be responsible is to know that our perceptions create reality, so we can either have a limited perspective, or a global one. When we believe we are limited, the world is also showing its face as limited, and when we believe we are infinite expressions of God, the world will show its face as likewise, just as the alchemist realized. His perception was his mirror, and it showed him a cosmic truth of unity. When we are responsible, we accept that our perceptions create reality; so, we take our choices seriously concerning each situation we find ourselves in.

Its efforts reach down into the hearts of humankind and awaken their power to transcend themselves and set aside their own egoism in order to feel the sadnesses, challenges, and sufferings of all people. Through the power of moral intuition, we recognize that it is morally wrong to act in ways that will hurt or harm another human being because we ourselves would not want to be hurt or harmed in any way. The setting aside of the ego is what is key here, since all our patterns identify the false self as the delusion; there is great power in this rule being able to undo the egoistic patterns of humankind and stop the patterns that make the false self, seem real. We will only attain peace when there is purity of heart, when the mind is free from egoism, the "me" and the "mine". It is not possible to conquer a person who is pure of heart. There is deep wisdom in the saying of Jesus in Matthew 5:8, "Blessed are the pure in heart, for they shall see God." There is a space of awareness of no-self that arises, and this is exactly what we must find to alchemize our inner Being and awaken the light within so that we can drop the false self and identify with the true self. The false self is the illusion, the dream that we must overcome and transcend by identifying with something greater. When we identify with another human being, our sense of self has become greater. We transcend ourselves and immediately know our love expands infinitely.

What is characteristic of the Golden Rule is empathy. You must feel what it is like to be the other person. This is the realization of one's own humanity. It propels a journey of open-heartedness to others. Oneness is the outcome. Here wisdom and love come together in the mind of the aspirant. When you feel that you are treading in deeper waters, you can always feel that there is a way out when you have an open heart. This is the place of trust. Trust is the foundation for all healthy and happy relationships. At the heart of this experience of switching places with another person is the letting go of one's self and identifying with someone other through this space of love and trust. It is a process of becoming one with all people that is moving, and this leads to world peace efforts and peace within. Empathy, therefore, is an expression of our being who we most essentially are.

Can you take a step back from your own mind to understand the greater picture? You will be affirming that there is a way that I can relate to another person. This is beyond questioning that the other person is alive to the truth that you know. It means that love has become the way of the prophet and you will see with your eyes an untold beauty. This is not an ordinary move for anybody, but an extraordinary move in spiritual intelligence. Spiritual intelligence is also called empathy and it gives you the power to transcend yourself and your limited perspective. You mind stretches into humankind and you put on the face of humanity. You can attain a state of unity, as the alchemist knew was real when he perceived himself in all people and knew he was one with them, based on his likeness to each one. You can know how to love when you take a step back, because you have stopped the superimposition. The Golden Rule gives you this power to become one with the universe around you so that you can truly understand the situation. This point of view is not subjective, but comes from God. It is God's eye that is revealing the right or wrong thing to do in the situation. For the alchemist to attain enlightenment, he had to step back from his own mind and identify with his new understanding of himself as pure, perfect, full, whole, and complete, and as being pure, unconditional love, and he said this identity was in all people. He conquered his own ego and became God. The patterns of the world were not defining his identity anymore, but the heavenly patterns of virtue were steering their course with his soul, which mirrored these higher patterns. For the alchemist to transcend his old self and the patterning of humankind, and in order to attain cosmic awareness, this required a state of total identification with the true self, and then it required becoming one with other people. When you learn to love one another, you will find that you are one with them. You have found the essence of the alchemist's power when you say "I am like you." This means that in an effort to find your truth, you can be compassionate with all other people, for they have the same truth that you know is real in you.

The empath awakens to the fact that he has found a way of oneness. The alchemist can find the love within, and so can the empath. In this way, the alchemist is healing human consciousness. This love is greater than when he thought he was in the old program. The patterning of humankind is based on limitation. This was removed by our ability to transcend ourselves and identify with the truth of another person and realize that his truth is the same as my truth. The thinking of the Golden Rule is in line with pure, unconditional love because, without conditions, we take the place of another person and love them as much as we love ourselves. Loving without conditions is part of your self-development. Don't believe your own mind when it says you're not intelligent enough, not talented enough, not whole, because your mind will lie to you and create love with conditions, which is the basis for you not accepting yourself fully. That kind of love only hurts you and others. Only when you love others and yourself unconditionally can you be set free. To get started on that journey, it is easy: follow the Golden Rule.

Can you ever take your life away from the way things ought to be? It is very likely this moral force is touching your love for all people. Love is the goal. Surrender. The past truths that you had within you will dissolve, opening up the space of existence for a new reality based on the love and acceptance of your self, and all people and creatures. The way the world works is that this old program of human patterning is going away.

See that the light that shines is you.

When one looks deeply into the matters of humankind, one may begin to discover answers to deeper questions related to oneself. Did you ever wonder, "Where did I come from?" and think it was greater than who you were? This question will take us on a healing journey, to the deepest recesses of human consciousness. It is there that we can find not only who we are, but what we came here to be. Understanding is fundamental to self-knowledge. A greater understanding of oneself can be the birth of a civilization, and when one takes hold of this greatness, it can lead to cosmic awareness. One does not need to have all the answers for the attainment of light. A child will beg his or her mother needlessly, for hours on end, simply to understand his 'own existence. It is there that the child can press into a kind of belonging that will take the soul to an even greater place than where it felt with family. You do not need to long for a family when there is a self-realization that is made possible in the undertakings of understanding the knowledge that "'you are the light".' Becoming what you are not is not possible with the eye of light. It shines in and through all things. Here the cosmic awareness can explore to include the realization that we are too like stardust. Waking up has never been so profound when we turn our eyes to perceive as if we were God. Can the world ever be this abundant? What was once taken as in your mind's eye as your self-consciousness can be readily made available in life without ever blinking an eye.

He who travels to the distant beyond will arrive in the identical place as the one who has cosmic awareness. Great is the mind that wonders, "Who Am I?"

Coming into self-realization is not only about pondering the truth within, but about wondering what it is that holds the world together, for the very same fabric of reality that holds the world together has mapped a coordinate power to hold our own minds and bodies together. So, by knowing the great truths of world coordination, we can ascend into knowing what harmonizes our life. This is a great feat, for it requires delving into the esoteric philosophies of humankind. What was once lost a long time ago can be rewoven into the fabric of our Being and awakened within. He or she who travels into the beyond must take this into consideration. We cannot expect to receive the answers to everything, but we can attain the wisdom to show us the way. This is what the light essentially does until you awaken to know that it is self-illuminating.

Way back when you were a child, you could touch this mystery with your mind. It is the essence of all things. The mystery of the great wisdom is that people are in a prison-house and must open the prison door to remove the iron fetters, and flee from their suffering. We awakened to hear the chatter of our parents, our siblings, our teachers, our pastors, and society and other people only to realize that the mystery was far less attainable as we grew older. It was not our failure to hold onto our childhood, but the revelations that came from our growth made it impossible. It is deeper than conditioning and patterning of humankind by social roles and expectations about ourselves that made coming into a better world impossible. The fundamental belief was that this world was only attainable in the beyond, when it can function here and now, without a myth. It is hard to imagine that you can touch this magical existence with your mind. This is called joy. As Buddha said, there is "everlasting Joy that had no enjoyer nor non-enjoyer". Joy comes from human connection. The worthiness that you feel is a product of the belief in yourself. Knowing you can be authentic is the potential to realize you are not to be abused. The system of abuse causes you to spiral into self-hatred, and it is the work of the true soul to say it can be forgiven. You will build deeper on your human connection with the Golden Rule.

Connectivity is not a burden.

Can the world ever be recovered from what was the downfall of the Noahide covenant? It is never too late to implement a world free from sin. This is what the Noahide covenant was attempting to do. The world free from sin is the creation of Heaven on Earth. Can this ever be articulated? It is not without trying that the major world religions have all attempted to introduce Heaven on Earth, but have fallen mostly upon deaf ears, except the Western civilization that gives the Noahide covenant Heaven on Earth.

When it comes to Heaven on Earth, you can be sure there are angels guiding your evolution. These angels have come from the distant beyond to ensure the development of your angelic features would be true. For what is Heaven on Earth without angels? The angelic features that you seek to attain are not possible without going through a transformation. This means shedding the old self by taking off the masks that are worn in daily life. This is called surrender and letting go. You no longer need to wear these false masks that constantly affirm a self-image of pain and untruth, which is based on vulnerability and fear. The pain that we feel as limited beings makes us commit crimes and sin against others and ourselves; so, we need to find rest. There can only be rest when you come to terms with loving and accepting yourself for who you are. You can live your life as if it is Heaven on Earth. The divinity that propels wisdom is you.

You can attain power by letting go of the patterns of resistance and struggle simply by allowing things to be as they are without judging them, or by liking and disliking. This power is attained by knowing the truth of who you are. Our personal power can be weakened when the codes, rules, agreements, programs, and patterns that we have adopted are wrong or even corrupted. They are wrong when they articulate an idea of untruth. The result is that we feel powerless. Most of our power is used to keep these programs running, when all we simply need are the five ways to sustain us. There can be a radical letting go of all the past programs that were teaching us to live a lie and a radical acceptance of the five ways of the wise, which teach us to live a way of truth. What can be claimed is that the angels have set this Heaven down for you at the time of Noah, and not to distrust them, but to look unto them as givers of life.

Where is Heaven, but within? When you turn inward, you can have the heart for perfect wisdom. So, you need to go within to discover the truth that Noah knew was possible. Where has the light gone if not into the Noahide covenant? It is there that we can find the grace and truth of the mission of the Lord. Do not go far from this place of rebirth. It was not a time that was inconsequential, but was given to humankind from the goodness of God to relive their truth of creation. Here is the way, the truth, and the life, which is what Noah knew was possible.

A simple governance is not what the Golden Rule is here to do. It is an effort in peace-keeping, yes, and so it is an effort of love. But it is a brilliant manifestation of a time of God-fearing. So, the ways of the wise are not just to be tried on, as you would try on the Noahide covenant. The soul is weak, but the flesh is weaker; so, the Golden Rule is there to strengthen you. He who turns up the way of life, as Noah did, can see that this first way is included in every world religion. In essence, it is the way, the truth, and the life itself. God is the creator of each and every rule and ethical code in world religion. So, we can count upon the creation of our own mind to be perfect. We can count upon it to be known as truth. When we try to learn about ourselves, we can gain access to our truth even deeper by searching world religions. It is a great gift to have this knowledge. It can lead to discrimination of the truth. By far the greatest love on the planet is God. What you are attuning yourself to is this love. Building yourself up is not just the joy of God; it is the purpose of His creation. The world religions have declared the five ways of the wise to be accessible to all. This creation is for the mind of all people.

Coming into your truth is about having knowledge of the Golden Rule. This can wrestle people away from the death that people find themselves in on a daily basis. The lostness that we feel is catastrophic. Losing yourself, you find yourself. This is simple, but profound wisdom. This is not what it means to know yourself. How is it that you can be fueled inwardly if you don't have the Golden Rule? It drives us innately. The Golden Rule undoes the spell that we are under. The reality of each person today is that they are governed by a hand of God. We welcome the presence of a divine directorship in each of our lives. He sets forth not only the rules, but the ways to manifest life. He puts conditions on the planet. What drives our very motivation is not something that comes from within, but something that has been placed within. It is like the old story of the acorn that has within it the knowledge and the life to become a tree. So, nothing can stop it from realizing its fullest potential. It even has the power to circumnavigate if something were to try to kill it. This is essentially what the five ways of the wise are doing in your life right now, preparing you to be self-realized. Nothing can get in your way when it is the very codification of truth. The list goes on and on about the number of codes that are accessible to humankind, but there is a place to stop when we need only the essential teachings, when we need only what's fitting. The governance of humankind is a giant code that has been placed in our hearts by the prophets, but there are five ways of the wise that show the way. Returning to the world as it is today, we see that there is much confusion over who gives governance to what, so knowledge is scarce. This can be seen as a planetary fate that we must try to stop. We can only succeed by asking that the fountain of wisdom overflow to all people so that they may quench their thirst with the same wisdom that is given to us here.

It wasn't that long ago when it was commonplace to wonder how to make the world a better place. This can be accomplished by living the truths that have been passed by for centuries. For when we start living these truths, we can manifest the reality of Heaven on Earth. When we begin to realize Heaven on Earth, the world can be healed. For a long time, people have wanted to stray from the programs in their mind and their ego patterns. The ways that you will learn are fitting to create a reprogramming. It will create a shift in your awareness, and this shift will constitute a rebirth. You will find yourself transformed. Given that these ways are told from world religions, you can trust that they have a proper life with them and it is the truest form of life that you can get.

Before the Golden Rule was passed down from the sacred wisdom to this generation, there was often thought to be emptiness. The darkness we feel in our mindset is really the world shattering our true selves. But know the cup can be filled with wisdom. The truth is that the five ways of the wise contain the essential wisdom needed to transform your life for the better and cause you to master your life and attain freedom.

The world program is different from the personal program. It's about education in the world program, but in the personal program, it's about self-centeredness. The world program gives you a deeper calling on your life than the personal program. So, we can't eliminate that there is a world to consider in our daily life. The world that people consider to be theirs is not really theirs. There is a world that they are losing sight of, yet it can be regained with the Golden Rule. What the world was when you were younger is the same reality in the Golden Rule. The ways of the wise represent the fountain of youth. They represent the eternal dream of mankind. That is the hope that we will realize, a rest from all evils. That is possible now that the five ways of the wise have been passed down. We can look to these ways as the benefit of all humankind. It is undeniable that God was present in the one that communicated these ways. So, we will never stray far from His life when we begin to follow them. They are the water of eternal life that has been promised to us. God did not fail when he wrote these ways. He triumphed.

What would it be like if all people followed the Golden Rule to master life? There would be a world peace movement, and this would lift us up to creating Heaven on Earth. There will be no more emptiness when all humankind is allowed to prosper. The planetary dream of mastering these ways is not just possible through self-truth, but in the effort one can make in becoming one with God. This quest is not self-defeating. For it is shown here that oneness is possible. The call to become greater than you already are is what is fulfilled here as well. You can learn the way of mastery easier with the five ways of the wise. This involves the tireless effort to become one with God. But what is mastery other than life? Yet many people are afraid to live this life and have a fear-based mentality everywhere they go. Where is it that you can go, if not to a sacred text for understanding? When you wonder about love, life, truth, there is no real discussion about how to answer these questions, but with God's thoughts. Looking back upon the past you can see that the programs that pattern your reality with roles have been insufficient for you to run your life. It is time to tune into your truth, and then the veils of ignorance will be lifted.

There is a universal code of ethics revealed in all world religions consisting of a few universally accepted rules. The origin of these religions is found in the truths of these ways. A person that holds these rules as a universal code is called an ethical universalist. They claim that there are some moral judgements that are true everywhere and they remain the same for all moral agents. They make the minimal claim that for whoever holds only that there is some moral judgement or other, that goes for everyone, rather than saying that all moral judgements go for everyone. What the ethical universalist needs to show is that there is a least one moral code that holds for all people. Perhaps the most common universal ethical code you may think of is "'Do not lie", yet there may be exceptions to this ethical code. The one code that was agreed upon by all religions is called the Golden Rule. To be an ethical universalist, you only have to agree that there is some kind of action that is always right or always wrong. This rule not only seems right to our moral intuition; it can be understood as well.

The Golden Rule has the power to stop the patterns that imprint our souls with the marks of subjectivity and relativism. It has the power to remove the outside dream that guides us away from the truth of a universal code. With it, you can find a different life. What you think was your divinity was a calling. This is the point of your transition to transformation. Your calling is your innermost joy. Living the life that you have always imagined requires doing the work. Then you can find your place in the stars. This can mean that the dreams of a new world are alive in even the mind of the pioneer. It was never too late for him to find a stone.

Your mind is at work all day long. It's constantly talking about a greater reality. So, you often hear in your mind that you can be greater. This is the essence of humanism. Simply walking down the street, you will become alive to the greatness around you. This greatness can be taken apart by even the scientist. He will show you that he has a way of reality that he is processing, and he needs the effects of humanism not to die. The greatness cannot go outside yourself. You need only to apportion yourself to the dream-making properly. Your mind belongs to an eternal world when you are touching upon these truths.

When you've taken the veil of illusion away, you can find that the ways of the wise are real. These dreams can become a nightmare, so they have to be healed. It was a grand illusion of the Masters of life to call yourself mortal, when in fact, you have the power to be alive for an eternity. The illusion doesn't allow us to know what we truly are. We have to look deeper into our mirror and recover our true selves. This can be a product of knowing the Golden Rule. When you know the first way of the wise, the illusion can dissipate. This illusion is the manufacturing of your ego, if you have not yet said, "I am here." When you fail to see your own presence, you will suffer. Life is not just an illusion. There is a way of the wise that is found in all things. That way of the wise is real, yet there is an illusion that you have to be aware of. It is the mindset of everybody to say, you are down. Often, we are depleted when we find ourselves in the illusion. When we touch the illusion, we have to affirm the truth in our lives. Knowing this, we can shut out the source of depletion and be made to be more aware that there is something like energy. This is what you are. When you constantly affirm a negative stereotype, you will find yourself without energy. You have to come back into your life by saying the five ways of the wise are my ways. Turning over a new leaf is something that all people do. This brings us to the point of knowing that there is something that can be found. It leads to a greater state of awareness when you find within.

When you have conquered yourself through purification, like the alchemist, you can say that you have been transformed and you can hold onto the eternal universal reality more easily. Life with alchemy is a whole transformation. The means of transformation is to look at the truths and say they are mine, so you can be accountable for your actions. The force within you is not to be reckoned with; it is to be made accountable. When you feel that you have found your truth, know that it is part of the way of the wise. When you learn to adapt to every situation, you will awaken. This is by not reacting, judging yourself, feeling sorry for yourself, and comparing yourself to others, but by simply abiding in the present moment. You must stop the fighting to simply abide. The way of the seeker is to know that there is no limit. There only the greatness of infinity. This predicament that we find ourselves in is called the illusion. We must rise above this illusion and rise above thought to go into the greatest love possible.

The way is truth itself. This is the way of light. Sometimes you can't know the truth distinctively, through the eye, ears, nose or mouth, but sometimes you have to ask, "What is the way?" in order to realize what truth is. the way is questioning. It will inspire within you a blossoming in which you can foresee the world in the flower itself. It's a precious thing within your heart. It is like the eye of the soul is the seer, in which the seen is beheld in the power of seeing. So, don't think that you can't look within. The world within is for you to behold. The truth is there for you to know. So, go for it. Don't withhold your experience of the world. It's there for you to know. It presents itself for you to be known, so you can be in it and enjoy all that is. You can overcome the darkness with the five ways of the wise. The light inside is also what Jesus was talking about. Soul is the impermeable. It is not the mask that you put on. It is not the world within, but the world itself. It is not "'here",' nor "'there",' but always "'in between".' It is not what you wear, but how you can say, "I am that I am." It is undying. The truth be told, it is forever. Never once will it go from you; always will it remain. It is at home where you are. If you don't know that it is your truth, then you will find it eventually. Consciousness is a light inside you, and that light is soul. What can be made of yourself is that which can be shown to be alive, and that is soul. There is a light inside the soul that you can use to awaken with and steer your sight towards the truth. Never before has it been tarnished.

When the tide turns, as it often does, where will you go when you find out there are people worse than you?

When you feel alive, this is when the five ways of the wise are really working for you. Wisdom will turn on as a fount. The five ways of the wise have an effect on all parts of our lives. We have to find them within, and we have to do this by studying sacred texts. The greatest revelation is knowing that the five ways of the wise are here for you. Love is what the alchemist is ultimately trying to achieve. And this love is also for healing the planet. He who finds the way within will find the way of love. Did you ever want to go beyond the world and know you could transcend your situation? When you awaken, you will find the power to look into your soul deeper. There is a gem that you can even find that will show you that life is really in the present moment. You have to escape the illusion once again, by knowing that you can be here and not in the drama. When you know there is a way of the wise, you can find the way of light. This is caught up in the way you use language, for the truth is that language can act as light that produces the truth of what is, or language can act as darkness to hide the way of the wise. Remember the story of the two roads. The prophets knew about this when they wrote about the light that you can attain by shattering the illusion and removing the veil. The light that we all seek to attain is in the alchemist's mind. The first way, the Golden Rule, is regarded by the alchemist as his way. He can talk to the dreams and say, "They are mine." These dreams become part of his care. Often our dreams are corrupted from the language that harms us. It places our mind outside the universe; so we fail to see that we are the dreamer, and the dreaming is what is happening right now. But the mirage can be lifted so that we can transcend as Jesus knew was possible. Transcendental consciousness allows you to stop identifying with your limited self, and to identify with the inner wholeness.

There is within the fabric of self-consciousness something that knows reality is made of dreams, for it propels the soul into the light. The mind becomes muddied by the projections of other people; so, it must be purified by language. Language acts as a filter to purify the mind, which is like water and can become pure in its original nature.

But what is the mind? Is it the mountains, rivers, the great wide earth, the sun and the moon and the stars and everything, so that what you think, you become? Your mind is the truth of there being an instrument within you that operates like a tool, as a sculptor has a tool and chisels out a design from the marble using the way of design, and in this way, your thinking operates like the chisel, forming the thought's desire. Most of our thoughts are petty and continual and do not reveal what the marble is revealing, that it is a whole being in the marble and this whole being is the tower of thinking itself, so we need to control the tool better to form with the chisel properly. The most perfect thoughts are those that are controlled by the chisel, while we often fail in perfection, and this causes us pain. We are typically going from thought to thought. This is the essence of our minds. This question is the desire for truth and a thirst for realization. The tool within you is a tool for transformation.

This gives you the chance to dream a new dream.

You have come into a great design when you consider the Golden Rule. It is a design of human engineering that can transform your life. This new program that you seek to tune into is made available to all humankind. The soul of humankind is awake to this transformation. When you know the truth, you can be a master of all things. Knowing the truth is knowing what is reality. The truth is we have all heard the saying before, of how words and concepts can get in the way of reality and how our desires, preferences, and the reasons for them can stand in the way of reality. The Golden Rule has the power to help you see things clearly. When you are not seeing things clearly, you are experiencing needless suffering. You will think the rope is a snake and not a rope. Reality will be something that can bite you and harm you. The Golden Rule goes much deeper than the words you are reading. With effort, it helps you awaken to the truth of who you really are and help you be your authentic self. The Golden Rule can open your spiritual eyes. The result of following the Golden Rule is the complete love and acceptance of who you are. That means, you stop judging yourself and others, criticizing yourself and others, and stop comparing yourself to others.

The dream-world is not just full of stars and galaxies. It is the world that fails to mention that there are fixed patterns of reality that are different from the ego's patterns that define our selves, our cultures, and our reality. It is these fixed patterns that the alchemist knew were real. He found them within himself and within other people. He then began a quest to show that they existed in the world. For him, they defined his Being as pure, perfect, full, whole, and complete. These patterns mirrored the patterns of God, and he was God to all people. Yet the five aspects of the original self are intertwined into the dreamworld and they must be disentangled through knowing truth and identifying with the truth of who you are.

When you are set free from human patterning, you will be your natural self. The soul that we wish to alchemize is made perfect with a universal morality.

Can you ever be awash when you know that every religion has agreed upon it? Looking back upon the ages, we can see that the way we were was not right until we had a universal morality. The reprogramming of humankind has to eliminate the latent subjectivity that is built into ethical systems. Looking back upon your life, you can see that your life was not complete without a universal code. The ways of the wise can create the most beautiful reality, with Heaven on Earth.

The Giver of Life planted a seed in the minds of all humankind. This seed was planted into fertile ground, and it could produce abundance if watered properly. The soil had to be rich to nourish the seed. It was the seed of life. It was promised to never be corrupted. So, it was the fulfillment of God's plan to allow this seed of life to become full, whole, and complete, shaped in the likeness of God. Thousands of seeds are planted over your lifetime. They are opinions, thoughts, ideas, and concepts and they are planted in the mind, which is fertile. But it was not long after that the seed of life lost its fullness, and the way of reality was not piercing the truth. So, it became corrupted and empty of the fountain of youth. This meant that all human beings had to suffer. Love was not even possible to heal the brokenness of the seed of life. But the five ways of the wise have taken the seed of life back and have placed it in a fertile soil called the alchemist. So, it would not become undone in humankind any longer. This seed of life can grow and be nourished by the five ways of the wise. Any one account of truth will pierce the veil. Going into the depth of the alchemy involved, you will take the seed of life away from the enemies, so they will not be able to steal the glory of the light. There was a war going on in the alchemist's mind that would take over even in the dream-world and plunge him into a state of chaos, which would unfurl the energies of life. This would cause the alchemist's mind to deplete from the seed of life so that there was no home for the innocent. But with the ways of the wise intact, you can call back these energies like a magician. You can use your mind correctly, rather than stupidly. The alchemist had within his mind the seed of life the whole time so that he could be aware of the comings and goings of chaos. Life could be replenished if he could learn to use the five ways of the wise for his self-transformation. This involved taking the Golden Rule and applying it into the seed of life. The seed of life could be replenished by these actions. There was a journey that all people could take back to a time of their childhood, and this was being replenished as well. This journey is not complete until we understand that all the ways of the wise are making an effort to heal your soul. So, the journey can again be set among the stars. The seed that you planted in the beginning of your life is being healed by following the Golden Rule.

God planted the seed of life within the heart so that it would become fertile through the wisdom of alchemy.

When you are following the Golden Rule, you create your own Heaven; when you do not follow the Golden Rule, you create your own Hell.

The extent to which the first way of wise is real has been demonstrated by world scripture. You can never go wrong when you appeal to the prophet. What he has taught us is to transform ourselves into light. We can leave behind the false identity that came from the wrongful identification with the false self. This has to do with leaving the false notions about what is "'me'" and "'mine'" behind. What we know in truth about the Golden Rule has been shed light upon by the ancient wisdom. He who knows the true self will know the first way of the wise. There can't be another way made possible when there is a universal ethical code. Knowing this will transform your life.

The Second Way of The Wise:
Listen with Your Heart

The second way of the wise is listen with your heart. This is so easy to understand. Listen with your heart. This way of the wise was formulated by Saint Benedict who said, "Listen carefully and incline the ear of your heart."[14] Whatever you are experiencing in life, listen with your heart. This will help to change the world within. This is your coming into alignment with compassion. As soon as you stop listening with your heart, you are trapped by the ego's patterns that condition you to believe that you are only your mind and not your heart. You can only escape these patterns by listening with your heart. This will elevate your soul to a higher world where you be reprogrammed with a new program based on love, purity, and perfection. Coming into your power is about listening with your heart.

---

[14] Stories of Encounter: Pray Now Devotions, Reflections, Blessings and Prayer, edited by Hugh Hillyard Parker,

There are many factors in the search for wisdom. Let's consider listening with your heart. Love is a great wisdom.

The heart has been placed in the center of our Being. The true self is centered in the heart. It is the seat of the soul, the place where you encounter God and enter into the bliss of paradise. The wise person that follows the path of the heart values the values of a quiet mind, rather than noisy mind, intuition, rather than deduction, and lives entirely in the present, rather than the past or the future. The heart is not like the mind; the emotion of love is not like our thoughts.

What then is love? Love is the essence of there being a God that has caused your heart to desire the things that are good, true, and beautiful, and in effect, it is the awareness of the goodness, truth, and beauty of God Himself. This means there is no evil anymore in you when you love. Love is an activity of the soul in which the two become one, and the oneness is complete. It is not just a passive expression, but an active expression of choice, desire, and the conscious fulfilling of a promise of the heart. Love is undeniably a field of energy that you partake in, and you can share in God's greatness by being part of that field. Love can place within you God's self so that you may not feel separate and invisible anymore. Taking on your soul journey is about listening with your heart. Seek the truth in this new place.

When you discover your heart, you can touch the great wisdom.

The heart is patient and has no desires. What brings about the patient heart is the listening itself. This will draw the mind away from the mental clutter of the outside world into the serenity of peace, but only with patience will you be able to draw that serenity into your life. And your wisdom will increase. It is like the aspect of your soul that is giving birth to something greater. With patience, you can erect the foundation needed for the alchemy. This transposes your mind from angry to peace. So, you lose the innate sense of evil with patience. You can bring about the thought of yourself more quietly with a patient heart. Your efforts to know the patient heart will be highly regarded in your mastery. When you feel the anger coming around, you must recede into patience. Adapt with non-action and tune into the deep wisdom. It is about trusting the way itself. We can leave behind the sicknesses of the mind in the opportunities that patience gives us. It is a never-ending love with patience. Respond; do not react.

The heart has no self-images, nor does it seek to defend itself, withdraw, escape, or protect itself, like the ego, which is a multiplicity of self-images, roles and characters that play their part in the dream. It has no enemy, nor shame or guilt-based self-distortion, which often defines the ego and motivates the striving of the perfectionist. It is not constructed or projected but exists within the body as a space that the eye of the soul can enter through the flowing of spirit. Thoughts should serve the heart. You are not your mind. The wise person thinks with the heart, rather than feeds into the creation of a false self. This is the path of love. Love is the nature of the pure soul; it is without impurity, taint, and spoil. It is without conditions. It is pure, unconditional love. That is what you are. This is your true identity. The thoughts fueled by love purify the mind and destroy the wicked works of the shadow self. The heart gives us life beyond all measure. You can never feel entrapped when you go with the heart. This is the way of love. You will become unaffected by and uninvolved in the sins of the world. The selfishness and lack of humility that most people feel can be counteracted when they focus on the heart. Here is the way you can be free from the self-limitation of the mind. You will not project your pain when you are in your heart. Your pain will be healed by the love that you find within you, and this is the love for all people. When you take the path of the heart, you will stop the mindset that pushes you to your limits. These limits are dissolved by love. The mindsets you typically have are different from the mindsets you have with the heart. With the heart, you know you are free from the mental distractions that only serve to remind you of the past programs of the false self. Listening with your heart shifts your perspective to love immediately. You will respond with love, not react from the unconscious patterns such as fear.

When you have an experience of listening with your heart, you will have an experience of no-mind, for what was happening in your mind will be non-existent. The patterns that you perceived in your mind will die. In meditation, this is often where people find their peace. Listen deeply. Do not be hesitant. There are always more worlds within. Should you feel suffering, just listen with your heart. Being great is a product of this power.

What we all desire in our lives is a deeper connection to our hearts. The feeling of losing your heart connection comes from human patterning. It causes fear, suffering, and internal conflict within the self. The drives within the mind will tell you to want something here, and reason will tell you another. We have to let reason rule over the appetites and desires of the body, or else we will find that we will lose our presence. Listen with your heart. When you harden your heart, there will be a loss of wisdom. When we do not listen with the heart, we will suffer. This empty feeling we have within our minds, is always a feeling to find the heart. You can never be set free unless you know the path of the heart.

Your wisdom of the heart lies in finding this gift of the silence within. This is all that the saints preach about. It is your life. Here is the silence of the heart. It comes directly from God's mind and it can tell you that the silence is the stillness within. You are part of the ocean of Being. And this is the attainment of peace. Eastern wisdom contains the element of stillness. As Buddha said, "The greatest goodness is a peaceful mind." You cannot be more silent than when you have seen through the dream by listening with the heart. Silence is the foundation for discovering truth. Deep within the recesses of all philosophers is the impenetrable way, and it was born from silence. Socrates, the wisest of all men, spent most of his life contemplating and remaining silent. Silence is the way of the wise and it brings fruitfulness to the philosopher. The wise person has a quiet mind and valuing solitude, consciously enters silence to discover what the reality of truth is. By staying focused on the quiet within, you can heal. We know how Socrates would go off and stand motionless, and "how he would start thinking about some problem or other, then just stand outside and try to figure it out. If he couldn't solve it, he wouldn't give up, but simply stand there, glued to the same spot."[15] Sometimes he would not leave until the next morning. Learn to be silent. Silence is the foundation for discovering truth.

How can you find true silence? Live each day in peaceful contemplation. Truth is revealed in the silence. Can you feel and hear the truth speaking to you in the silence? The truth you feel in the silence is God. The way is to drop the inner chatter, so that you can find the way of reality in you. Coming into your true self is like knowing that you can be present in all things. This is called self-transcendence.

Your mind will be settled instantly when you feel the heart. This is calm, and you can directly know yourself when you listen to the wisdom of the heart. You have to trust yourself; then any choice you make will be correct, but if you do not trust yourself, anything you do will be wrong. Listening with your heart removes the social mask of ourselves and anchors our Being in our true self. It is the way to be truthful with yourself. Since all pain is associated with the mind, you will find that, by listening with your heart, you will let this pain go because the pain itself is an attachment to something you desire, crave, want, or lust for. These build up into the mind and say that you don't have anything without me. They can be let go easier when you listen with your heart. Take heart; this

---

[15] Symposium 175c-175; 220c-d, in Plato The Complete Works.

is the way of the Masters. Deep within you is the call of wisdom.

It's not the external self that is alive in your life. It's deeper and more powerful. There is a soul that says, "I am here." Just as we thought, we can be free. You are the gift within, not the person outside doing things. It was not something that could be hidden within an eternity, for God had placed the right way within you so that the gift could be found. Coming into this truth is called awakening. It's as if there is a sun that shines there for you to know that your self is different from the external self that wears the masks each day. It takes courage to unmask the false self and know there is such a great love there within. Love is like the soul itself. It is your true nature. Knowing the soul as it is in truth will resolve the inner conflict and organize the soul by reason and with the virtues of wisdom, justice, courage, and temperance so that you can discover what is real and genuine. The greatest truth attained by following the wisdom of the Masters is this: you are pure, perfect, full, whole and complete. Just say, "I am that." Attaining this truth is a spiritual victory. It is the most vital step on your way to enlightenment. The travesty of being caught up in your life without knowing the truth is like rummaging through emptiness. You can find Being by listening with your heart. Say good-bye to the false self.

We become entrapped by the ego because of the feeling of pride. This is a feeling of superiority of the ego. In Ecclesiasticus 10:15 it says, "Pride is the beginning of all sin." When we hold onto ourselves, pride is the belief that we know better than God, and even better than other people. This feeling is the basis of selfishness, and not love for the self or love for others. The world becomes about "'me",' rather than "'we",' when the truth is that our world contains all people and not just our own selves. When someone says something to you, just listen with your heart to all that is being said without judging yourself or others, and without making comparisons between yourself and others. Listening with your mind makes you vulnerable to feelings of pride, while listening with your heart attunes you to selflessness. Why are we trapped in pride? We learn from human patterning to love with conditions. That is the way we love ourselves and the way we love others. We often say, "I love myself if I am a winner, if I am talented, if I succeed," instead of loving ourselves unconditionally. Love is not lost.

The way of listening with your heart is something that almost all religions have in common. For example, in Christianity, in Ecclesiastes 11:9-10, it says, "Walk in the ways of your heart and the sight of your eyes." There was a way that Confucius said this: "Do not listen with your ears, but listen with your heart."[16] In the Sutra of the Great Accomplishment of the Maitreya in Buddhism, it says, "Listen attentively with one heart." There is a completeness that you know is within every heart within the Buddhist tradition. In Native Spirituality, this way is expressed in a poem:

If you listen close at night,
you will hear creatures of the dark,

---

[16] Daoist Meditation, The Purification of the Heart Method and Meditation. By Wu Jyh Cherng, p.

all of them sacred —
the owls, the crickets, the frogs, the night birds —
and you will hear beautiful songs, songs you have never
heard before. Listen with your heart.

Never stop listening.
~Henry Quick Bear, Lakota[17]

There is nothing greater than he who finishes first in the category of wisdom.

When one listens with the heart, one can find the ways of the wise ever deepening. Deep within our soul, we confront ourselves and must face reality. It is not hidden from this ear. What it will teach you is the magic of the dancer, and the dance. This dance is part of the moral code that we talked about. Love was not written out of this dance, nor was it excluded from the totality of the way. It is a grandiose move to know that you are part of the dance. And where it leads is to the home within the home. Surveys can teach us where to find life, but only the dance can teach us to be life. At once, you will awaken and know that it is about tuning in. At last it can be brought to your awareness. As suddenly as you can say, "I am here," you can find that you are the real thing that you are searching for. This real thing is the light of all there is. It is life on planet Earth as well. Welcoming this attunement is what you need to do.

---

[17]http://www.spiritual-quotes-to-live-by.com/100-inspirational-native-American-quotes.html

In Judaism, there is short parable that reveals the power of the heart. It goes like this:

"Rabbi Yohanan ben Zakkai said to his five disciples: 'Discern which is the proper path to which a person should cling.'

After thought the first said: 'A good eye.'

Another said: 'A good friend.'

Another said: 'A good neighbor.'

Another said: 'To one who thinks about the consequences of his actions.'

The last said: 'A good heart.'

Rabbi ben Zakkai said, 'I prefer the words of the last, for in his response is contained all the others.'

At another time Rabbi Yohanan asked his disciples: 'What is the thing a man should avoid most in life?'

Rabbi Eliezer said, 'An evil eye.'

Rabbi Joshua said, 'An evil friend.'

Rabbi Yose said, 'A bad neighbor.'

Rabbi Simeon said, 'One who borrows money and doesn't return it.'

Rabbi Eleazar said, 'A bad heart.'

Rabbi Yohanan then said: 'The words of Eleazar please me most because his thought includes all of yours.' "[18]

Rabbi Yohanan ben Zakkai was considered the greatest rabbi of his generation. There is something to this ancient wisdom. Not only were there five disciples present, but they specifically spoke about the heart. Rabbi

---

[18] 365 Spirit: A Daily Journey For Your Soul, by Aaron Zerah.

Yohanan ben Zakkai turned to the most powerful example. This taught him to be conscious. This is the way of the heart.

Life can only get better when you listen with your heart. There are many examples of being absent, of when people find themselves neglecting each other's lives. This causes more suffering than once realized. When you turn away from the activities of the mind and listen with your heart, you can conquer yourself. This listening will take you into a higher reality where you can overcome your struggles that you find on a daily basis. Life can become complicated, but when this higher place surrounds you, it will be your love. You must quiet the inner self by tuning into a higher reality.

You can be deeply connected to truth when you listen with your heart.

Listening is the mind saying to itself, "I can be present." The heart speaks to the mind and tells it that it has to be present at all times. When the tides have turned and the listening mind is no longer present, truth is lost. There are glorious things that can be found when you tune into your heart. Listening with your heart is the way of Masters. It can bridge the gap between knowledge and ignorance. When you turn your life over to a higher power, you can find it within your truth that you are the listener. The voice in your mind seems to be you because you have identified with this voice all your life, but when you focus on a new space of awareness, like the heart, you can see that you are not the voice in your head. This voice is not authentic. The voice is authentic only when you speak from your heart. Continue your journey in this space.

Why is the heart so distant from so many people if it is the way of the wise? This is sad in the consciousness of humankind that people are so distant from each other. Love can always be found in the listener. When you have made the conclusion that you are alive with other people, as the Golden Rule shows us, you have to overcome this sense of distance, or it can lead to alienation. Alienation is the suffering of the masses. When you stop and think that you are alive with other people, you have found your place as the listener. This is the one that is not doing the talking, but the awakened "'you'" that hears the truth and acts on what is true. The awakened "'you'" is the true self. When you find that you are saddened by the ways of the world, you can always find power with the voice within that speaks the truth. This ability to find power is the awakening of the heart. It is the place of power itself. Your life is not stable if you can't listen with your heart. The prophets knew there is a way, and that way is always found within the heart. The key factor is that there is no voice in the mind when you are watching your thoughts as the witness. So, you have dropped the mindset of the old program and awakened a new program that comes from truth. You can find your Being when you awaken the capacities of the heart. Tuning in is like tuning out the world. Be prepared for a shift that will take on Heaven on Earth.

The parable of the Blind Men and The Elephant reveals that there is something greater that we can access. This is what the heart is revealing. You can find the way to listen with your heart is by stilling your mind. This is your inner sense. You can know yourself when you become aware of the heart. You were destined for this place a long time ago when you were a child. When you listen with your heart, you can find the pulse of the universe. Something within your life teaches you that you need to listen with your heart. It is innate so it can be accessed more readily. This way is about giving and receiving. You are going to receive love when you listen to the wisdom of the heart. Your way is conscious awareness at this point.

Finding your heart-space is finding the way of the wise itself. It awakens the revelation that you have a true self that is not your mind. You have come this far to being a self-realized being. And now it is the time to be made aware of what you are. Here is the knowledge. There is only one truth, and this is that the Divine is unfolding within you. Coming into your soul truth is like an astonishment. This truth was placed within your heart a long time ago. This is the life-changing experience of enlightenment. The transformation that you found when you found the five ways of the wise is not beyond your grasp. It is within reach. Heaven has sent love to be revealed in the greatest of people. You cannot be put aside when you are love. This is called Brahman according to Hinduism. This is what you are and have always been. Goodness is the virtue of love. Knowledge can't be found without turning your soul. Do not be afraid of what God has put in you. It has been called the greatest of all human emotions. Thus, you can perceive greatness with love. Putting on your soul truth is equivalent to you identifying with this power. Looking for your truth just got easier with knowing that you are pure yourself. This purity is not tarnished by the outside world. Great is He who has put this love within you, so you know that you are what is perceiving, and not the perceived. Soul is your original nature, and this love can enhance your nature. Be real; it is the only thing that is true for you. Given that love is your true self, you can always be real, even at the most inopportune moments. Giving an expression of love is the right thing to do at all times. Your life can become greater with this wisdom.

He who is angry does not realize that love is the true emotion of all the human species. Coming into your self-knowledge is about accepting this truth. This is the destruction of ignorance. Do not waste a second of your time on something wrong, but spend all your time being consumed by love. Give yourself a chance to be sensed as love. Knowing you are real is not undermined by anything. You have not been given a chance if you do not realize that this is the truth of who you are. It is not an absurd finding of your soul. Then you will perceive that you are alive with wisdom. Coming into your soul truth is the experience of Being. Do not be sad feeling that this is more than you thought of yourself.

Love is typically with conditions. The soul that says, "I will love you forever" pauses and insists there will be consequences for this love, but there are no conditions to the love that you are. So, you can let go of the false pretenses. Every other kind of love is with conditions. I love you if you will help me here, do this for me, please me here, say these things to me, then I will love you. That is love with conditions. What has been called a condition negates the truth of what you are. God has given you this purity without conditions. This is the real way of loving one another.

In love, there is only perfection. There is no attachment, lust, greed, pride, deceitfulness, hatred, or delusion. This is your space of realization. Being is the space of existence and manifestation. This is the space of awareness to know the truth of who you are. Take the time to realize that the space of awareness is really here for you. You are the reality of this space. Give yourself over to the knowingness of being real. The greatest of gurus will tell you that life is love and love is life. This is of course not what people realize on a daily basis. Often their minds are consumed with the ego patterns of hatred, greed, anger, and delusion. Love is the awareness of your life. Here, you can experience Being, which is the truth of who you are. Do not let it depart from you, the love that you found within yourself. Courage is what it takes to hold onto this love. Peace is what love also is. Be uplifted by this truth. Congratulate yourself on being able to identify yourself according to the way the alchemist sees it. You have come this far to know what is real; so, embrace it. Then you will feel bliss.

The energy of wisdom is fueled with consciousness of there being wholeness.

The way to end suffering is by showing people how to listen with their hearts. When you listen with your heart, you will be able to say, "I am not longer in the ego." This means that you must listen with your heart and find within yourself the love of wisdom, which will propel you to a higher space beyond the ignorance projected by the illusion.

Circumstances may arise one day that delay you from carrying on the search for self-knowledge. How can you carry on? Love yourself. Then you will be inspired to carry on. When an argument has not yet reached a conclusion, the wise teacher Socrates testified to this self-love when he said, "This is the alternative I choose, that it is for my own sake chiefly that I speak and ask questions and reply."[19] The followers of this ancient wisdom know this as truth, that only the love of the self can inspire the search for the true self. You must do things for you, solely in knowing that it is worth finding the diamond within, and you are the diamond. Then you can carry on with this self-love. The self-love that you feel in the first way is demonstrated by the second way of the wise. In your heart there is the capacity to hate, and rebuke the light, and this will show the way of evil, but when you find within your soul the love for wisdom, this will inspire your self-love even deeper, because you have chosen to find yourself out of love for yourself by choosing to ask questions that will shed light into the darkness of ignorance.

When you listen with your heart, you will stop identifying with the limited view of yourself and find yourself in the infinite waters of the ocean of pure Being. The old programs and old ego patterns of thought that the

_____

[19] Rep. 528a.

human mind finds within itself have to be shut off, and a new program of love has to be started.

New values have to be consciously chosen and accepted for a new program, and a new pattern of life will form. These values include affection, acceptance, friendship, caring, family, kindness, peace, loyalty, sharing, and service. You can drop all the ego patterns when you consciously value these values. Listening with your heart will be the effect of saying "I am here." This will give you a state of pure presence. You can detach from the mental chatter that occurs because of the monkey mind, which is always judging oneself and others, feeling sorry for oneself, and comparing oneself to others. When you get a grip of the monkey mind by listening with your heart, the mental chatter will stop, and you will find peace within. For what else is listening with the heart but peace? Your motions in your mind always pull you away from your heart, but by valuing your values, you can concentrate on listening with your heart.

The reality that we said is truth can only be found within the heart. When you find your inner guru, he will teach you all the ways of the wise. Just listen. The guru's voice is his presence. This phenomenon allows him to transcend time and space. The guru's voice is in each situation. You must listen to hear the voice of the guru. This is love. Then the guru will be in your space, regardless of time-space reality. The guru will be there, in a timeless, space-less space. He is there even when he appears to not be there. The guru is communicating to you through the space of awareness in each situation. When you pay attention to the voice, you may get a sense of aliveness and a different awareness, self-awareness. Notice what is happening in this space. You will become aware of the difference between the feelings of awakening and the normal feelings of the dream. When you notice your thoughts, body, emotions, and other mental states, you will feel a sense of aliveness when you practice listening with your heart. That means that the guru does not exist in a space but exists as space. *Akasha* is the Sanskrit term meaning space. It also means sky. It is lovely to think that the sky is with us in each situation — we are drawn into the expansiveness of space and even into the heavens — but not so lovely if there are clouds. The greatness is hidden. We must seek the greatness.

Ask and you shall receive. Seek and you shall find. Knock and it shall be opened unto you.

Just listen. That is how we must search for the sky. If we hear a bird sing, do we not turn our eyes upwards to the sky? It is the same when we are searching for our true self. We must search through the cloudiness of our own egos and know there is a blue sky hidden within the clouds. The bird sings, and we drop our egos and just listen. The sky is closer to us when we listen to the birdsong. So too, our Being is closer to us when we hear the voice of the guru in all situations. When you sit with a guru, you must learn to sit still, even for hours and hours. You may feel pain in your legs, but this too shall pass. There is a space within you that is pain-free. Even that space is the guru. It is the space of the heart that remains free. This is where the eternal, immortal, indestructible and blissful you, exists. You need only believe that you are pure, perfect, full, whole, and complete. This is the place that all people ideally want to be, beside their guru. He is wellness for all people. By far the greatest thing a guru can show you is how to listen. When you begin listening to your thoughts from your heart, you can touch the mind of the guru. This is because the thoughts will be coordinating a new program for you. These thoughts will be pure, because they have not contacted the false self. They will be powerful as well.

With increased devotion, you will awaken the voice of the inner teacher who is a source of guidance and strength, and who can lead you further inward to your true self. As you worship, so you become. This is kindling of your spirit. Knowledge comes from lighting the intellectual fires of truth that are burning within the eager soul, not by pouring facts into an empty mind. Everything that you once thought about is not self-taught, but learned by the way of education. Can virtue be taught? Virtue is not a measurement you can do within yourself; it comes from a true belief that there is a "'you'" that has rarity within that can become a philosopher and by recollecting this truth when the teacher shows you the way. And you are the light that you find in your heart.

Life has a way of slowing you down, so you must keep up the pace.

When you listen with your heart, the eternal world is governed by a new dominion. This dominion has the code of law already in it; so, it cannot be tarnished by moral relativism. When you aspire to something with your heart, you will escape moral relativism. It will not touch a pure heart. You will come into contact with your soul when you listen with your heart. It will make you more aware of the present. In this place, you can find the love of God. This is a quest for divinity, immortality, and bliss. It is a quest to become like God.

You can attain higher levels of truth with deeper listening. This will bring you closer to God. When you feel that you have lost a part of your life, there is only one way, to listen with your heart, to recover what you feel is lost. When you come into contact with your love, you will be filled and overflowing. The second way necessarily works with the Golden Rule. The ways all work together to form a new program that is birthed through a new awareness of being like God, universal, cosmic, and greater than you ever imagined. It is like seeing the elephant for the first time, knowing that before your perspective was limited because it was created by human patterning and spiritual blindness. All ego patterns can do is create a limited self, but divine patterns can place a seed of eternality into the soul, and you can find your eternal self. Ego patterns are limited in nature. Divine patterns are unlimited in nature.

When you learn to remove the patterns of humankind, you will find there is innocence. This is because your Being will never be harmed by human patterning. It remains uninvolved and unaffected by each system of human patterning. It remains pure. Human patterning has set cravings very deeply in the human mind; so, these are the patterns that will be deleted. This way of the wise shows you that there is a purity and truth that is not lost. This is why the five ways of the wise cannot be dismissed. You will learn to detach from all falsities when you follow the five ways of the wise. They are there to set you upon the stone of transformation, like the alchemist.

Coming into your divinity for the first time is what the Masters are going to teach you. Following in the footsteps of the Masters is the way of God. You must imitate their character so that you can emulate their righteousness. There is nothing you can't find in the teacher's way of life because he has attained the limits of perfection. They had a higher form of consciousness. This was built into the fabric of their precepts, law codes, and rules. Listening to the Master is like listening with your heart. Look no further. The Master was situated in your heart a long time ago.

Will you ever feel beautiful again? Looking into your own mind is not what listening with your heart is. It's the conscious movement to a new life free from human patterning. You will consciously release all the old patterns that were put there from parents, siblings, educational systems, religious orders, and others, and receive the divine patterns that were set there for you a long time ago. Ego patterns have no truth because they do not value what the heart values. Love is what the heart values. You can get left behind if you can't find that listening with your heart is the way of peace. You have to consciously undo what was done to you in your childhood and upbringing. By knowing yourself and pure, unconditional love, you will switch off these mental programs and delete the patterns that reinforce your false self. When you find your true self, you will find that you can talk with your heart as well and place within your heart your mind so that you can continue to rewind and release all the old patterns. When you have your consciousness in your heart, this opens up the space of truth. This is the way of meeting God in your mind. This meeting is the healing of your soul. God has given you a heart to be conscious. That is what the heart is for. We just need to believe in our true self. Live as if you're going to die. You can turn up the volume of your heart-space at any time.

It is human nature for human beings to imitate each other, when all you must know is that you have a divine nature. Therefore, the Path becomes a way to imitate God and to assume the same likeness as God, being beauty, wisdom, and goodness. When you know your divine nature as truth, you will stop imitating others, cease from judging and comparing yourself to others, and the false self will die. You will feel the growth of your wings and soar aloft to the higher realms. This will be your moment of freedom in your angelic form. When you move into the truth of the higher realms, you will find that you are detached from all of life's agonies. You will learn this more deeply in the final chapter on the Path to Freedom and Self-Mastery.

The truths found when listening with the heart are undeniable. They are passed down by the Ancients in prophetic scripture. They give us the motivation and inspiration to hold onto what is called a universal truth. They propel us beyond indifference, into love. Awareness is the first step into transformation. It gives you the power to be in the present moment and identify what the truth is and what the lies are. When you know what the lies are, you have to remain in your heart to listen to the secret wisdom. It is there that you will receive the truth again and again so that you can constantly break out of the patterning of humankind and find a new self, born again with the power of love. Your encounter with death will lead to rebirth, as the Mystery Schools teach in the ancient wisdom traditions of esoteric philosophy. This power that you find within cannot be taken away by even the lies, even though they try to have a hold on us. The lies that we live with today have to do with the conditioning of the self as a limited and often imperfect being. This imperfection is not true when we hear the voice of the Master remind us of our true selves. The Master is only found within the heart.

Your consciousness cannot be taken away from you. It is the light within, the light behind the mind that shines to illuminate the thought-forms and gives you the power to perceive the difference between the true and false selves. It requires a constant remembering of who you are, in your truth, by conscious awareness of the path to the sanctuary of the heart where love exists in infinity. And finding yourself there, you will stop the inauthentic voice that constantly projects the false reality that you are not good enough, not talented enough, not smart enough, not pretty enough, and not perfect enough. With the knowledge of the second way of the wise, you can be set free from this false reality and learn to love yourself again. Self-love is what it takes to put on a new self.

The second way of the wise gives you the power to awaken the human potential within. This has the truth of limitless possibilities and endless opportunities. It is the truth of the way of love. Love is the essence of the second way of the wise. In 1 John 4:8, we learn: "God is love." The drug industry will come to an end when we propel the truth of Christ higher.

Know your truth.

You are the love you are searching for. This way does not shy away from the claim that everything is God and God is everything. This way of the wise is divine.

Whatever happens around you is divine. Love is the motion that is propelling the divinity. God has called this divinity Himself. Life is the divinity that you seek to realize.

This second way is sacred. It opens up your soul to the truth of the Divine flowing through you and through all things. You can find your power in your divinity. There is evidence of the Divine all around us. This makes it possible to become aware of the Divine within us, and possible to become aware that the ways of the wise are divine ways. This is part of the wisdom. Knowing that there can be a divinity within all of us is why we are here. Here is the truth of your divinity. When we begin searching out an answer to the question "Who am I?", we find the answer lies in knowing that there is a power within each soul, and it grows to infinite expansion, and when we contact the love within ourselves, the same principle found within the Hindu, in which they conveyed the Godhead as Brahman, showed there was an identity within the individual with God that was effortless to see in the ways articulated by all these other religions. When we love ourselves, we are not exempt from this knowing.

There is an aspect of your own self within the story of creation. It tells us that we have a divine sign within us. We can always find divinity in our creation in the Book of Genesis. We may find that beginnings are obscure at times, but knowledge has shown us that we can understand beyond the obscurity. When we go through this, we can find that life itself has been fortified by the five ways of the wise. This has to do with the building up of the soul within the self-consciousness, not tearing it down. We can use the fortification of Taoism to strengthen us. It teaches us that there is a way, called the way that we can find as truth. This has also to do with Adam and Eve. In the story of creation in the Holy Bible, these two beings were situated in the heart of God. This makes it possible to have a meeting with the Divine. The heart is the place of this union. There was a dreadful time that God knew was going to happen. It would shake our foundation and cause us to die. Our death was from our disobedience. We were told not to eat from the tree of knowledge of good and evil, and we did. And this collapse was the end of our heavenly state and the end of our truth. Dread in the mind of God moved human beings to save themselves, but that is not the answer. Instead, the answer lies in the power of the crucifixion. There is an overwhelming sadness that came from the crucifixion of Christ. But God gave us the power to be reborn. This is the power of the alchemy of the philosopher. There can be a rebirthing process for all human beings if they want to enter the kingdom of Heaven or realize heaven on earth. Your old self must be reduced to ashes, including your dispositions, your false beliefs, your self-judgements, and your likes and dislikes. As Buddha said in Sutta Nipata 1072-76, this is "when the person has gone out." This is possible through acknowledging our divinity. Through the inner transformation of yourself, you can rise like a Phoenix from the ashes.

Coming into contact with your Being is attuning yourself to the divinity within. All humankind has a divine nature that is pure, perfect, full, whole, and complete. This nature is non-injurious, non-hateful, non-violent and not evil, because at the root of this goodness is God's love and His spiritual *logos*, which is truth. Christ is the *logos*, or the Word. In John 1:1 it says, "In the beginning was the Word, and the Word was with God, and the Word was God." This truth will keep the realization that you are to be moved not by the forces that cause the mind discontentment, disturbance, and chaos, but by the greatness that you can hold on to with a love of all Creation. What God's will wants, is for you not to be lost, but for you to be found. It is not just by following the spiritual *logos* that comes to you, but by opening your heart. God's will can invite you to know who He is, and then you can follow His wisdom better. When you find the spiritual *logos* preaching to your life, do not go too fast, lest you lose what is beneficial to you. God has granted for you to know Himself. This is done through the depth of fire in the alchemist's mind. Fire can bring you into love. It can set your heart ablaze for God. Revealing the divinity in the way of the wise is about finding the fire so that you can find the love within.

When you feel the programs of your past have started to harm your life, there is only one way that you can heal, and that is by listening with your heart. You can let go of all human emotions and find joy. Joy is the result of listening with the heart. When you have gone away from your heart for a long time, there has to be an attunement so that you can be once again listening with your heart, not your mind.

Coming into self-realization is the end of self-judgement. You will learn to be in this space, free from all error. This includes the identification error in which we identify the ego as who we really are instead of our true self. This is the greatest obstacle to enlightenment. When you have touched upon this reality, you will find that God is with you and you will listen more deeply. When you find yourself in the heart-space, you will realize that listening to the world's sacred texts is in the same space. It does your heart well to know what the prophets and wise have said. God is alive in these ancient texts; so, He becomes alive in you when you listen to them. The way of love can teach you to let go. It can also teach you to be patient. These are the ways of divinity within us all. Do not go far from this moment of grace, for it brings you into the presence of the Divine. This is the cause of all our undoing; so, we can be real. What it takes is for you to know the ways of the wise are changeless because they reflect the eternal perfect patterns of Heaven on Earth. Heaven on Earth is a power to heal your soul.

There are traces of divinity in all the things that God made, but by far the greatest traces of divinity are in the works of the prophets. These traces give us the power to perceive the original nature, for it is revealed in each bit of evidence that God had a name for us. So, we don't turn our backs on Creation. The forgetfulness of our divinity is the reason why we suffer. This creates an illusion of separation, and although we can grow from suffering, the pain of separation causes us to have unhealthy attachments, desires, and sustains the ignorance brought on by an identification error, all of which cause us to hate and commit evil. There was dread in the mind of God when he heard Cain kill Abel. The power of this moment has never been healed in humanity. It is not without effort that we can believe once again in the greatness of humankind to rectify this grievous sin. The power of sin is intolerable. We are ignorant of our divinity. When we find the downfall in humankind, we will be able to make a difference. This causes us to hurt ourselves and others. Just as you know that you found your life by listening with your heart, you know you can find your life by stilling your mind.

Can there ever be a release from the bonds of suffering? What is the way to end suffering? Since ignorance is the bond that creates the sorrow, the way to end suffering is knowledge. Reclaiming our truth is about overcoming these bonds. Perfection is equivalent to the idea of the way of the wise being divine. This is the truth of who you are. Remembering the truth of divinity within all things is the power of the ways of the wise. These ways have been given to all humankind to assist them in their path of wisdom. Walking a Path is part of the way of divinity.

When you find that you can make peace with all people, you can find the divinity within the second way of the wise. By making people happy, you will find peace. When you arrive at this place in your Being, you can focus on the divinity of reality in the eternal moment of now. Your capacity of finding the divinity depends wholly on this ability to make people happy. This demonstrates your capacity to love. Have you ever wondered why you can't maintain a long relationship? It is simply because you can't maintain your being present by saying, "I am here." So, your mind drifts to other places and you lose your state of presence with the other person. This causes unhappiness, and suffering. When you can learn to love yourself, you can learn to love another person. The capacity for self-love is endless. This means you must treat yourself with care and kindly, as well as treating the other kindly. When you find the self-love within yourself, you can awaken from the dream. Healing has to do with knowing yourself as well as loving yourself. You can always find your way by knowing something sacred. Take back your life today.

The second way of the wise, listen with your heart, is part of the way of spirit. It is by valuing the value of spirituality that you will be able to master this way. The evidence of something spiritual is the evidence of divinity. This value is linked to other values of spirituality such as peace, authenticity, intuition, wisdom, peace, forgiveness, and mastery. Life is spiritual. Listening with your heart is not only physical, but spiritual. Are we spiritual beings? The reality of life has been attuned to the spiritual since the beginning, and it encompasses the psyche or the mind; so therefore, what we do in the spiritual, we also do in the physical.

Listening with your heart physically also includes and appeals to and demands listening with your heart metaphysically as well. Listening with your heart means accepting your responsibility of Being. This means that we can conjure up the way within our own minds. The depth of our spirituality impinges upon us so that we will go forward in each physical endeavor more carefully. We can find that in the motion of conjuring, there is a sense of gratitude that we feel. This superimposition that we spoke about earlier will be destroyed with this kind of talk. When we think of the spiritual, we necessarily involve this act of gratitude. Love is worth finding.

Here spirituality is not so far away from you. The religious dogmas that we talk about reinforce your spirituality. They are complete in their effort to be made accessible to all and show a triumphant call to know that the spirit, which is an effort in the calling, has not been lost. Here the rise of conglomerates has in effect, supported our spiritual quest in their effort to tell the tale about the movement of humanity. In documenting this spiritual quest, we feel that we can turn our lives over to a higher power more readily in the West than in the East. When we submerge our world into a Way, we can find the rise of totalitarianism weakened. There is a global thought within this new transformation because it is built on something all-encompassing, and therefore it sheds light on the fear that we felt as a child. The child growing up in the West knows how to find freedom. It is not just a gift. It is inherent in the play of forces; so, we triumph with the knowledge that we have attained. The fear of the child is what is driving this spiritual quest. So, the perplexity is not found any longer when we know the way.

The world that we are trying to understand is the one that God created for us to be perfect. This has to do with knowing the world scripture more than anything. The five ways of the wise can solidify our beliefs so that we won't be programmed into a daze. Taking the divinity away from most people is what the world does. The five ways of the wise can put this divinity back into your hands and hearts. Grace is the cause that will save people in the coming of the Messiah, says Christianity. This is the element of hope. We place our minds into something unheard of before that can be materialized into our mind and body. What we need right now is hope more than anything. It transfers our lifestyle into a God Mind. It demonstrates more than belief; it demonstrates faith. And that is what we are missing from this modern age. We need faith more than anything. Faith is the power of a belief in things unseen. We place faith in the coming of the Messiah because we have hope that he will save our souls. This takes us into an existence of God more than anything. We can stay in that existence for all time, according to the promise of God. When God fulfills His promise, this is an act according to the second way of the wise. He is love, and because God loves us, promises are fulfilled. The promise fulfilled has the element of grace. We cannot go far from His presence if there is a love coming to us at all times.

The program that needs to be deleted from your mental awareness is soullessness. This is a condition of agony. The pains that you felt in your past can be healed.

You just have to accept that this is the love coming from knowing the ways of the wise. There is a place beyond the place of wonder called the way, and by knowing the ways of the wise is where you can begin your healing journey. Knowing how you began your soul journey is how divinity can be found. The way of grace shows us there is something divine in the movements of reality. Truth be told, listening with your heart is an awakening of consciousness.

Listening with your heart is being able to resonate with your highest joy. If you can start listening with your heart, you will find the freedom from all disturbances. No evils can come into contact with you, and the mental poisons will dissipate. You can see how important this way of freedom is. Just by practicing this way, you break the patterns that kept you trapped in worldly suffering. Listen with your heart. As you make a habit of listening with your heart, you will learn how to take responsibility for your choices without guilt and self-judgement. When you truly understand how to listen with your heart, your heart will be set free. You will abide in a state of bliss. Coming into conscious awareness is a life abundant.

There is a harmony within you that preceded the harmony without. The ancient wisdom of Plato calls this "a song of life".[20] It's a song that you don't want to miss. It spontaneously attunes your soul to the soul of the universe, taking you deeper into heavenly realms, away from the captivity of the mental chaos where you can

---

[20] Rep. 532d.

enjoy the sounds of life flowing to you and through you, welcoming you to experience the wholeness, completeness, and oneness of the endless rhythm of life and love. Love is the first principle of movement. Be spontaneous. It is the song, the singer, and the singing, and when you attune yourself to the singing, you will transcend the divide between the subject and the object and realize it is "'you'" that is searching for yourself that is being sung about. The ways of the wise are music to your soul. There are musical moments with each turn. The teacher's voice is music to your ears. The sound that comes from the Masters' mouths is intelligible and clear, distinct and true, deep, and resonant. The sound is a soul attuning itself to life. A song that is sung is the working of the Tao, like a story that is told. It holds your life together. It is beyond comprehension the way it can say, "'I love you.'"

Some people will say, "I'm always going to listen with my heart," and they will set the intent consciously, yet they will forget the next day, and lose their heart connection. Do not worry; as your awareness grows, you will remember the ways easier. This is what the five ways of the wise do; they increase our awareness. Be gentle with yourself. Like any practice, it takes time. Go for it.

As you think in your heart, so it will be true. By perfecting your thinking with the five ways of the wise, your thoughts will not be disrupted by falsity, nor muddied by attachment, nor stained by indulgences, nor made impure by passions, nor ruined by bodily desires, nor soiled by illusion, nor disordered by wandering, but will become perfect; truth will be your reality. Your heart is not born free, but a cause of freedom. The love that moved you to think in your heart is what moves the alchemy of truth. This is the same as self-love. Becoming free is now becoming more of your reality. Your soul will be healed in this journey.

The Third Way of The Wise:
Focus on The Present

The third way of the wise is focus on the present. The journey to focus on the present is long-awaited. We have a tendency to live in the past in our lives, but this is not the way of the wise. Whenever we live in the past, we find that the truth of our soul is diminished. We plunge ourselves into a drama and feel suffering. It seems the whole world is ignorant of the present, so this is the cause of our unavailability. We become free from suffering just by focusing on the present. This can transform you in a profound way. This way of the wise, like the others, will give you your power back. Love will reach you in the present moment; so again, it is a focus on love. Usually we live our lives based on past experiences or future predictions. We fail to focus on the present. It is always better to focus on the present. This will create your healing. The illusion of the world is built on the past, but shattered in the present. This is because we dream up the future and hold onto past dreams, but the bubble pops, and we lose our sense of self. The dream is not possible in the present. Stay present in your own Being to be who you came to be.

Living in the past is the cause of so many problems. We expect things to be the same as they were in the past, or we expect the world will conform to our dream, but this is not the way the world is. So, our real self is lost without focusing on the present. The past that people focus on doesn't have anything that people can change. So, your will to live dies. When you find your reference is the future, you find you always listen elsewhere other than your heart. In the present moment, the mind can find the opportunity to love. In the era of temporality, wisdom will shut off, but in the era of life, wisdom is eternal. Here is an example: you decide to get a new job and change your life by moving forward, but each step you take brings you back into childhood pain, so you end up not being able to change your life and move forward until this pain is healed. When you focus on the present, this pain is dissolved and you are set free. The past has no hold on you when you focus on the present. Focusing on the present frees your heart from difficulties that we have with others and have with ourselves. Continue your journey with this way.

Like the previous two ways of the wise, the third way of the wise also has evidence in sacred texts. In Matthew 6:34 in Christianity, it says, "Therefore do not be anxious about tomorrow, for tomorrow will be anxious for itself. Sufficient for the day is its own trouble." In Psalm 118:24, in Judaism, it says, "This is the day that God has made. Celebrate and rejoice in it." In the Lotus Sutra verse 5, Buddha says, "I know the present world and the world to come as they really are. I am the All-knowing, the All-seeing, the Knower of the way, the Opener of the way, the Preacher of the way." In The Gleanings from the Writings of Bahá'u'lláh in the Baha'i' Faith, it says, "Verily I say, this is the Day in which mankind can behold the Face, and hear the Voice, of the Promised One." Taking back your knowledge is about turning on the fount of wisdom. The wisdom that you need is found in the ancient scripture. It brings the power of the prophet into our lives. Here the truth that is within you will be substantial.

The love can't be lost when you focus on the present. In these world scriptures, one can always say the love is real. Sometimes the envious face will appear, but there will be the real face outside the envious. But it is not in the beyond where these world scriptures are. It lies in the fact that they are here. Wisdom is enlivened by the study of world religions.

Love is only real in the present. What you have found out about yourself is that the ways of the wise can only be known when you say, "I am here." Focusing on the present is your accountability to the truth. Within each person is the soul of accountability. The feelings you find within your heart are the moments of focusing on the present. These are the times you say that I am not talking to myself, I am only Being. This is the essence of who you are. The truth that the world religions knew about the present is what you can find in your life. They are telling you that there is something great in the moment of now. When you find this moment to be real, all of the past dissipates. When you find your space of existence, you can always refer to the five ways of the wise and say, "This is why I am here." Your purpose is in the present.

The third way gives you the bountifulness of your soul. Life is very difficult if you cannot access the present. It presents you with hardships and trials and errors that you cannot solve. Pain is very real in every moment, but when you access the present, you can take your eyes off the unknown. There is a pain response in all people. It teaches us to like something and governs our category of thought. This unknown factor is the soul wanting more and craving more and not being satisfied until it has these things. This sense of attachment arises when you are not present. When you stay present, you can end the agonies of the attachment. You will be practicing detachment from the wants, lusts, cravings, and desires.

The coming into conscious awareness is by focusing on the present. This is your chance to awaken into the truth of who you are. When you find the present moment, you can find your stillness within. This is the place that you can find your love. The love within has never been this real when you focus on the present. There is no time and no space in the present. There is only the endless, limitless, boundlessness of freedom. The path to freedom is what we are here to discover. Your way is not always the right way. This is the path of the inward healing journey. To be set free is the goal of all great people. This has to do with stopping all the unconscious forces that set our minds adrift in suffering. Focusing on the present is an effective technique that you can use to still your mind.

The first step is become aware of the space of existence in which you can focus on the present and to consciously affirm the present over all the mind chatter that constantly projects a mental world from fear. The unconscious forces cause you to go away from the present. By being present, we can maintain conscious awareness over these forces and learn to speak, think, and act from deliberate action, not from an unconscious force that causes us to react. In the present, we can respond, not react, and this can bring the light into your relationships, family, and work life. This means that we stop and think about the object of our awareness and separate ourselves from this object instead of immediately identifying with the object. Without identifying with the object, we have the time and space to find our heart connection, but when we immediately identify with the object, we are lost in the mind of suffering. When someone is causing us to feel angry, without staying present, we simply identify with the anger and become it and react from anger, but by focusing on the present, we can separate from the emotion and take an objective view of the situation without reacting. You don't know who you are when you are reacting, but you know who you are when you are responding. The fights and the battles can then stop, and you can return to a place of peace and calm. We suffer when we get angry. By considering that our space is really the same space as other people's, we can infer that they too are suffering. When someone hurts you by judging, offending, or insulting you or by behaving violently toward you, this inference makes it possible to see that the person is suffering as a result of his own anger and own violence. But by being angry at the other person, we have violence within us, just like the person that hurt us. We can act from compassion and stop our anger and violence. As Buddha said, you can conquer anger by love.

The third way gives us our power back to respond in the present, instead of reacting without thinking about it. There are no thoughts that arise when you focus on the present. This practice stops the mental chatter, clears the mental clutter, and controls what Buddhists call the monkey mind. Can the mind turn itself off more than by focusing on the present? It is there that the end of realities of the past will be determined. You will find that the stillness within calms the emotions in your life. This is the release of all suffering. When you learn to let go, you can learn to stay present. Other values associated with the present include calmness, peace, caution, attention, control, discovery, authenticity, observance, vitality, and solitude. We must value the values of the present to practice the third way of the wise.

For the alchemist, attuning himself to the present is the care he can give to himself. The present is the idea of love itself. You can find the presence of light in the alchemist's story. He who wants to be in the light will always find it by focusing on the present. Love is where you can find the alchemy of transformation. He places his mind in his heart and says, "I am here." This is his testifying to his Being. The mind can move faster when you stay present. When you know yourself to be alive in the moment, you can be transformed easier. The alchemist can remove the damage done to himself by way of the human patterning. He has the power within himself to release these patterns by way of letting go. Finding the power of the present moment in your meditations is one thing, but you can focus on the present all day long; so you can find your way easier through life. This way is about listening to your inner person. It is the ephemeral appearance of the outside world that reveals that the inner person is long-lasting like a stream that flows beyond the outside world; without beginning or end it flows. It is the longevity of the inner person that has many causes and conditions; so, we need to remain certain. We struggle to hold onto this image of the stream, but it is the greatest image of mankind. We exist to fly. But we can find the inner person to be the soul in the ancient wisdom of Plato. The whole of human civilization is programmed to stay away from the present. It starts by valuing the value of the present. This will set your heart and your mind right. When you focus on the present, your mind is detached from the agonies of your past. This is the way to master life.

What the world has planned for you is greater than you can ever imagine. It has the five ways of the wise built in. The five ways of the wise are all characteristic of you becoming more powerful than you have ever been. You will realize your greatness when you choose to follow the five ways of the wise. They have the power of helping you break the patterns of humankind. You can deprogram yourself with these five ways and reprogram yourself according to ancient wisdom. This wisdom is like the elephant in the parable of the Blind Men and the Elephant. It may not be seen by all, because of spiritual blindness, but it is there just waiting for you to let the light shine to set you free from the darkness.

The five ways of the wise reveal the problem as self-ignorance and give you the solution for self-knowledge. Learning the truth about yourself is the most powerful way you can be set free. It gives you a new self-consciousness to identify with so that you can drop the illusions of the dream-world and stop being the dreamer who is trapped in the illusion of the self. The five ways of the wise are not relative truths, but shared wisdom. The universe and you are intimately connected.

We often feel how small we are when we measure ourselves against a mountain, a forest, the magic of a rainbow, the universe, yet when we focus on the present, we can feel a sense of belonging amidst the beauty and magnificence. This has to do with moving your mind away from the point of subjectivity to the point of the cosmos. You can learn to find your soul better when you know there is a universe with you. The present connects us to the universe.

Your universal consciousness is your reason for existence. It has within the dimensions of reality that you can contact for your wholeness. There are many dimensions that you can find simply waiting for your exploration. The power to explore is the power to remain present with the whole. This wholeness is you. You can find the wholeness in the simplicity of a grain of sand, as William Blake knew was possible, or you can find it in the ancient elders' talks, or you can find it in the commitments you make with each other, or in the revelations of eternity. Whatever path life takes you on, whether simple or deep, there you are, confronting yourself in relation to the whole at all times, but often we do not stop and take a moment to be present with the wholeness to feel it in our deep selves. We touch upon the Mystery only a few times in our lives, but these times are often temporary, as we long for something eternal.

You have likely heard of the eternal now. That is what the present moment is. It seems to last for an eternity because you have separated from your time-bound self and severed the bonds of past and future, which only cause us to project our thoughts into a space that is not real. These imaginings of the ego are the cause of suffering. The freedom from suffering comes from knowing there are five ways of the wise that you follow as your ways of life. They are very real means to freedom because they are born in the consciousness of wholeness, completeness, fullness, purity, and perfection. This is the consciousness of the true self. They are from the light; so by attuning yourself to the light, you can embody the reality of God and become like God in your characteristics and your thoughts. They create an ascension into the light.

The best way is to make these five ways of the wise your new habits, so you must break the patterns and habits of the old program and start the new program for your life. If you are going to start a new program based on the five ways of the wise, and build a new dream for the world called Heaven on Earth, reprogramming your mind is part of the process. It starts by making it a conscious part of your day to remind yourself that there are five ways of the wise that can help you master life and change your reality from suffering to happiness, from chaos to beauty, from hatred to love, and from anger to peace. Making new habits is not that difficult. Don't take everything as it comes, but go after what you want. Learning is simple when you focus on the present.

Write the five ways of the wise out on a piece of paper and put them on your refrigerator. That way, you will have a constant reminder of your reality as truth, rather that illusion. You will constantly remind yourself of the truths that can become part of your human consciousness by reprogramming your mind. These constant reminders of the five ways will delete the old programs of human patterning so that you can be set free from its mental traps. You will become aligned with heavenly patterns of virtue, not vice. Continuing is easy with this little trick.

Forming new habits takes conscious effort. It will not be overnight that you can start to think differently, but only through effort. It will take relearning behavioral patterns and learning to speak consciously so that you can avoid the suffering of the limited self that is called the ego. The ego is the creation of human patterning, while the true self is the creation of the new program and heavenly patterning. You can reprogram your life by identifying that these five ways of the wise are meant to do something good in your life. The reprograming process is like kindling the fire of consciousness. The five ways will uproot the self-images and social roles that we have that cause suffering, and remove the labels we have put on ourselves, such as dependent victim, angry tyrant, cursed, the oppressed, and helpless child. You wear these roles as the ego sees fit and play the part, as if an actor upon stage. Let go of these attachments; they cause harm to the soul. There is nobody else but the role that you can remain in, but the true self is the eye that sees the role. You will make a choice to affirm your authentic self, and the old self will naturally be dropped. Since the whole problem is that humans constantly forget their true selves, the reminder on your refrigerator will stop this immediate cause of suffering, forgetfulness. You will be forced to remember truth many times a day. The illusion will be broken each time you remember the truth. Your present is a gift.

The voice in our minds wants us to stay programmed because it is how we see ourselves in our self-identity, but this voice is inauthentic because it has been created by years of human patterning that took us away from the simple truths found even in world religions. These truths awaken our authentic voice so that we can learn to be ourselves fully and connect to something greater within. The feeling of remembering who you are is the feeling of light. This will dispel the darkness of ignorance. Without light, we are faced with spiritual blindness that will prevent us from ever seeing the whole of the elephant. Unlearning is a very powerful process.

These five ways of the wise are really simple, yet people will try and try and fail at learning them all. They may wonder: "Why can't I focus on the present?" This is because all our lives we learn exactly the opposite, and through repeated practice, what we learn becomes a habit. We practice the ways we learned unconsciously and automatically think, act, and speak from these habits.

Habits are so difficult to break. We feel that we will be safe if we continue our habits; so, they rule our lives. Look deeply into your soul when you focus on the present.

When you place your faith in a way of the wise, you will remove your faith in the unknown, which is precisely what the blind men were faced with and could not discover themselves. This causes fear; so, by reprogramming ourselves with truth, we can overcome fear. You must continue to learn the five ways until the entire program of human patterning from when you were a child has no more power over you. This is about you recovering your power that the patterning took away from you. With each label affixed to your self-identity, more and more power was drained from you, but with the five ways of the wise, you can remove these self-limiting labels and choose to believe that because your reality reflects truth, you are that truth. Proclaiming "I am the truth" is very powerful and can shut out the weaknesses associated with the limited mindsets. You can learn to trust your reality because it is based on truth, not illusion. The five ways of the wise are the perfect tools for self-truth. Go for it.

What we have come here to realize is that the five ways of the wise are the ways of all people. They cannot be removed from the consciousness of humankind. Once the programs of human patterning are released, we can all live better. The comings and goings of all the ways of the past can be dissolved when you think of the ways of the wise. The ego patterns have within their essence in-stability; so, you need to find stability in the moral doctrines that have been given to this world. The whole drama of the ego is dissolved when we focus on the present. The human mind says negative things all day long. That is how the human mind works. So, lifting your reality up to the present moment shuts the mind off. We are dragged back into the past from a need to feel safe. Fear prevents us from focusing on the present. So, we have within our mindset a self that is empty. This is what makes the heart long to feel acceptance and love. The sense of emptiness has dissolved when we focus on the present because there is no time or space for the mind to conceive anything. The mind forgets itself in the past and needs to be reminded of the truth. There is a failure in the mind to think in the past. This failure is a condition of human patterning that imprints a negative stereotype onto the soul. We believe these stereotypes because we don't have the courage to ask the right questions. We think that it is not safe to ask questions, and this too is part of our human patterning. The imprints show the soul that questioning is not proper, and we get punished for asking the wrong questions. He who has the courage to ask the right questions recovers the philosopher.

The heart of wisdom is philosophy.

The move to focus on the present is the move to stop the rejection. We have rejected ourselves because we cannot face the world. When we feel others rejecting us, we feel the patterning of humankind imprinting pain upon our souls. This is the cause for self-hatred and lack of self-love. We are reminded of the pain that we feel when the patterns take us away from our Being. So, we stop believing in ourselves. And this sense of self-denial causes us to be removed from our heart even further. We have to focus on the present. This will move us away from the imprints of our childhood. The move to love ourselves is the ability to focus on the present. Here the cause of love is stillness.

Where can we go when we have found the present if not into our heart? The love that we find in our heart is real only when we focus on the present. This reality is without blemish. Loving yourself is the power to need nothing. Holding onto other people's perceptions of ourselves is the problem of human patterning. These perceptions deny that we have truth within our life and they deny that we are here to love. This is the wisdom of the present: the ability to know ourselves more deeply. Hope is not lost when you focus on the present. When you have trust, you will find the present easier. You have to ground yourself and keep things real. Don't look back to the past; just focus on the present.

The mind tends to move in one direction, either the past or the future, but when you focus on the present, the mind is still. You can find the depth of your life within the stillness. This will bring you closer in relationships. So, when you feel as if you have gone the wrong way, you need to talk to yourself and say, "I need to be here," and allow yourself the power to drop the false self. This is what is called empowerment. Hold onto the feeling of the present, because chances are it will not last very long and you will have to remind yourself to practice the third way again.

The ability to practice is the ability to become a Master. If you stay with the practice, and keep staying with the action, your life will transform. This book is the introduction to a new way of life called true self living. Your way of life is essential to your social advancement. Love is alive with the Master. Hold onto the power that you find in the moment of the present so that you can be transformed by the renewing of your mind and by the restoring of your soul with the new program. Each day is a blessing.

Just imagine the day that you start focusing on the present. Your relationships will be transformed and your life will be transformed. Healing is a very deep endeavor that you can take when you focus on the present. He or she who finds the challenge, the responsibility to heal is greater than he or she who doesn't. Healing is what you can be realized in. This has the ability to release the soul into infinity where the soul is set free from all conditions of past and future. It knows no bounds and has no reality beyond the infinite. Being is the space of the present because it will entrust that you are here. Love is also the place of Being. Taking the idea of the past into consideration is the imperative of all wise people. God is closer to you in the present. Becoming aware of the importance of this way is the first step to becoming wise. It's a powerful thing to focus on the present.

When you focus on the present, there will be a self that is instantly accounted for in the universe. The message from the universe is that you are worth finding. The ideas that are presented here are not just important. They are part of restoring the seed of life. You can take back more from this idea and give back to the seed of life so that it becomes a flower. It is the flower of life that unfolds upon completion. This flower has been rooted in the fertile soil of human awareness. Accessing this truth is the power of alchemy. Your way is undeniably beautiful.

Focusing on the present is the endeavor to be quiet. This state of mind that wants peace brings you global consciousness and what we called global awakening. This is for the effect of healing the planet. The effort to know that the mind has a peaceful intention is the same effect that world leaders want. So, you have invoked world peace in your intention to focus on the present. This place of quietude is the place of impermanence. So, see the life that is passing you by is caught in the moment of the present. So, the web of illusion is destroyed, and all the foundations that talk about life being a battle are destroyed. Here the power of truth is revealed. The truth is that there is a democracy in the West and not the East. So, there is non-commitment to the stance of quietude. The lake that one part of the East stands upon is filled with ripples; so, we see that quietude is not there. There must be quietude for there to be world peace. Looking out into the lake of global consciousness, we find that the failures to bring about world peace are from the inability to love. Just as when John Lennon was promoting his music, there was quietude in his mind, but we have failed to remember our Being for this to be eternal. The end is near if the ripples on the lake do not find their peace.

But is the world in trouble that it will be the end of the world? There is a far-reaching significance of focusing on the present when we consider this in the light of global awakening. The world will become filled with greed, lust, hatred, and delusion only to the point of allowing this to happen. When the world population withdraws away from the illusion, the world consciousness will globally awaken and shift into the stance of the peacemaker and will say to the evildoers that the workings of the consciousness have to be made more aware. The stilling point of your mind is the end of evil.

We must do all that we can to enforce the stance of John Lennon. "Don't stand in the way of God's mind" is what we want to say, and it is heard loud and clear by all the world. This brings us an element of power in our music industry where we find the greatest expression of the human mind in the world. Turning away from global consciousness to our present moment, there is power in love. He who wanted the way of the world to be love was John Lennon. This reality is manifested when you focus on the present. John Lennon became the man of the world. So, we cannot go wrong by following him. Did you ever think that love was so far from you that you had to go back into the past to find it? He wanted his knowledge to be known by all. Stay true to yourself.

It is truly a journey when you have found the present. This is the inward journey that all people aspire to. This journey is anchored in the third way of the wise. Buddha claimed in the Sutra of Hui Neng 2 that *suchness* is the Master that knows the way. This is the power of the mind to say "I am that" and know that you are pure, unconditional love when asked the great philosophical question "Who am I?" So, it is not lost within the depths of being here now. The *suchness* is felt by abiding in the stillness. It cannot be moved.

There is nothing like the natural wisdom of the effortless of pure Being. It is the love of all Creation. Endeavoring to be this love is what the alchemist became, and it is your power to know you are on the same path. This is the path of purity, perfection, fullness, wholeness, and completeness. We think that John Lennon has the same qualities within his self-knowledge; so, we have found him to be truly enlightened. The power within you has been completely transformed by making this a habit.

Focusing on the present will take you into pure Being. This is another part of the mind of John Lennon. It is within his mind to know that he could abide in his own purity. Purity is what he gave to the world, and there is nothing that could remove this purity from him; so, it is his eternal self that sung those lyrics. Love was the reality that he promoted. In knowing that you can remain present in all situations, there is an abidingness that can't be taken away. This is called Being. It places the self of John Lennon in the world so that the world would stand up and take notice of the eternity of his self. This is the key of life. You can take hold of this key of life when you hear his music, and it will play the same eternality as when he was singing. This is because the point of reference is love. The self-government of all people is the present. The key of life controls how we should talk to one another and act in the world. This is what *suchness* is, self-governance. Governing thyself is not part of the monstrosity that you found within the ego. In the way of the world there was a power of *suchness*. This means that eternality is a rare thing to have and be given. There was none that compared to John Lennon's love for the truth. When we imagined the mind previously as a machine, this brought us into the power of where John Lennon really was. The sufferings of the planet were in his mind when he sang those songs so that it could be revealed to the world that there was a way of peace. The moments of peace that he created in the world are too profound to go unmentioned. Being accountable to the sufferings of all humankind is what we realize when we focus on the present. It can bring us pure joy to know that John Lennon was setting people free. He said, "Imagine all the people living life in peace. You may say I'm a dreamer, but I'm not the only one. I hope someday you'll join us, and the world will be as one."[21] These words reflect a global consciousness and global awakening that is even alive today. We can see the reflections of our Being within these words. Life is precious.

Remembering yourself is in the consciousness of God.

Use the key of life to attune the harmonies of the body for the sake of the concord in your soul, so far as you may go. Because there is a divine destiny for you. This means you are meant to discover your Being. You have forgotten why you are here, but the five ways of the wise will help you discover what was written in your heart. This truth is unalterable and perfect. There is a call to find your true self. A calling is what moves you to find

---

[21] http://www.keepinspiringme.com/john-lennon-quotes/

the potentiality for Being itself. Then you will find nothing wrong with you. You will transcend the lower, animal-like nature and to the higher, more perfect nature. You will even realize your angelic nature in your awakening. Can you shape your own destiny? There are decisions you can make and activities that you can do that can tap you into the consciousness of life, which is fertile and brings forth the mystical and magical powers of creation. This life carries a history with it and we cannot change the past. It is a false consciousness to think such things. This is the cause of pain and suffering. Life is worth living.

Life in all forms is imprinted with meaning, and this meaning is coming alive in a new way. You have not come from an accident, but from design. Your life has cosmic meaning. Your destiny is immortality, divinity, and bliss. Choose your genius. The life that you choose shall be your destiny. After studying the wisdom, it is up to you to walk with the Masters. Look no further.

For the end of suffering to take place, we need to focus on the present. The present is the constant reminder of love. It will arise in our minds that we have to care about more people naturally, and the miracle of transformation will start on our path. There is a need to transform. Built within the fabric of the human mind is a power to arise and conquer the forces of evil. When we don't transform urgently, these forces build up and threaten to take over the foundation of the heart and destroy the very works that we began on the note of truth. It is a time to be conquerable in the West and situate yourself without your mind chatter. The patterns that we said were existing in the ego show themselves in this need. The world needs to be healed. By healing yourself, you can heal the world as well. This means that you can be a vegetarian if you like, for then the world would be a better place. Looking into vegetarianism is all about reducing the amount of pain in the world. It will benefit the world for you to take this stance of non-injury to animals.

There is no more waiting in the present moment.

Truth is a call in your heart; so, when you search for the truth, you have to listen so you can understand that that which is meant to be found by you is alive in the present moment. Listen carefully to what is inside you right now. There is nothing other than the present moment. The truth is here for you now. You don't have to look for it. It is placed within your Being. So, you need to just remember that you are here.

The ability to remember your soul is the cause for focusing on the present. It is a cause from remembering. When you feel that you cannot focus on the present, the key is to remember something special within yourself. This could be a personal memory, or a soul connection, or the love that you always wanted. These aspects of yourself will be comparable to your real self. In the effort to retain these thoughts, you will have to place within your mind conscious awareness. Each time your attention is brought back to these aspects of yourself, you must remember that you have within your power a necessary ability to hold onto the present. Each aspect of yourself is like your life showing up for you. When you are not present for your life, you will, in essence, experience a death, and you will lose a part of you that was special. Here, we have the point of life being to love yourself. These aspects of yourself are not to be neglected because they define who you really are. The more we love ourselves, the more we can find this truth. But we don't need to look for ourselves too deeply, because we have the ways of the wise to show us the way. This means that you can enter this love at all times.

Looking into the past only causes our mind to go away from the present. This is the cause of our suffering. When we turn back to the past, we feel that we will lose our Being. You will lose Being if you focus on the past or the future. It is a constant reminder that focusing on the present is there to set you free. This means that your consciousness needs to be liberated from self-centeredness, which is the greatest cause of suffering. This is because there is total absorption in the self to the exclusion of caring for other people or even thinking about their feelings. You forget their importance as well. This causes great pain in the frailty of the soul. When you focus on the present, human angst will go away from the mind that constantly needs more things. This is called liberation from suffering. The disciple needs discipline and a strong effort to achieve the goal of liberation. The wise will seek liberation and detach from the old patterns of falsity, purifying themselves with truth. This is no different from what Plato wrote about when he described how the prisoners in his Cave Allegory saw the light for the first time. They were mesmerized by the particular objects in the sensible realm to the exclusion of knowing that they were real. So, they became afflicted with pain from the light in their eyes, and they went back into a cave for some of them. In the Tao Te Ching verse 41, it says, "the way out into the light often looks dark." So, the way of the light is to know that you can be set free in the realm of perfection, which is where the cave-dwellers were going to. You can find the light by focusing on the present.

The ability to focus on the present lies in the power of focus. This implies there is a center or a heart of awareness that we can attune ourselves to and achieve betterment in our lives. Often, we find ourselves focused on the outside world; so, the outside self puts on the masks and plays the social roles; so, the inside self is excluded from participating in the experiences of life. The external self-causes the drama and often forces us to stay focused on the play itself because the narrative of the life story captivates our attention and causes us to concentrate on different values, other than the ones within our value system, such as television, money, war, controversy, competition, and other such aspects of our drama. We lose focus of our true values very quickly when the external self is wearing the mask.

To change our focus, we need a reminder of the true and good aspects of ourselves so that we can recover our conscious awareness and our truth. Through the power of attention, which gives us the power to move away from the illusion and move towards a new space of awareness, we can become attentive to the object of our focus. This power is present in all people, but through human patterning the power of attention has been programmed to focus on limited aspects of ourselves. Values give us a new space of attention, and therefore a new focus. This is what it means to be more conscious. In essence, becoming more conscious has to do with our focus. When we start focusing on the truth within ourselves, we stop blindly following the programming of humankind, which seeks to weaken and negate our truth and causes us to be attentive to our dependency, rather than our self-reliance.

To get out of this problem, we have to take responsibility for our actions, including our action of attentiveness and what we place our attention on, because this action alone has the power to make us buy into the myth or to make the myth die. This, then, is the way out, to question everything. This is what makes philosophy so powerful in your self-transformation. It is also what makes philosophy so important.

When we ask ourselves, "What do we want to focus on?", we have a choice as to what we decide. Life is a series of choices. You are your choices. To choose is to be conscious of one's self. Happiness is a choice. Love is a choice. Charity is a choice.

Freedom is also a choice. Learn to come to absolute choice about what you are thinking and feeling. To take an example, when we choose to value our values, often one value is related to the other values; so, when we affirm wisdom as our value, this means we will have a host of related values to focus on, including learning, intelligence, education, and others.

Your ability to focus is your ability to know yourself. We must align ourselves properly to focus on the day. We must turn our focus away from the evils of the world, and turn our attention to the Good, the True, and the Beautiful so that each time we express ourselves, we express the true moral concerns that go deep into our hearts and into humanity. Here, the focus must be on creating Heaven on Earth as you live peacefully in this earth school and continue to manifest your dreams for the future. A focus acts to frame the picture you have of the world, and filter out the unnecessary aspects, and as our ability to concentrate deepens, the picture you have of the world is brought into awareness. Focus is key.

The habit of concentrated attention will help you arrive at the goals of the alchemist. This habit can be mastered so that your ability to focus is unwavering and the object of awareness is constantly brought into the picture you have for yourself. When you paint your picture, you can choose what to stay focused on. When you lose focus, you lose your picture and the world takes on the dream-like quality again; so we need to filter out these aspects by consciously drawing a line between what we value in our picture, such as authenticity, and what we don't value, such as lies, distortion, abuse, or else we will lose our authentic self. Think about it this way.

As children we are taught to focus on everything that makes us feel good as a result of rewarding good behavior; so, as we grow older, we continue to focus on these actions, failing to realize that we act unconsciously through habits, and we act automatically without thinking about it. The power of focus recovers your power so that you can act and speak by first thinking it through because a space of awareness has been created through the power of focus. This spaciousness exists in between thoughts and gives you the power to choose what to focus on.

When you choose to focus, you choose to recover your power and your freedom to paint your picture according to the way you really are. But life is not just a series of choices. Life is also the power within us to proceed from conscious awareness. Don't turn your back on this power within. The whole journey is really about focusing on the present.

Sometimes life can become complicated, but it was not all lost. It was just to be reorganized in the right time and space, which is here and now. This is the method that will never fail. He who practices this technique will know the way to self-knowledge was not lost. Self-knowledge is available to he or she who avails himself or herself of the five ways of the wise. Eternally you are here, but outside you are never looking. So, turn from the outside, and focus on the present.

Soul makes us conscious of two things, the way things are and the way things can be. Your focus can be placed on the way things can be. This means there is a moral "'ought'" in each stage of focusing on the present. But what is morality? Understanding the truth that morality is similar around the world, even within families and educational systems, is the first step to understanding the truth about the virtuous mind, for this reveals an ethic within humanity that demonstrates human perspectives are the same. This is because the truth of love is the same in the human spirit. The revolutions in human consciousness demonstrate that when we have an "'ought'" present, there is means for conformity. We can turn the tables on the strategist at any time. Life is not just about games, for there are many opportunities in the world to cooperate, not compete. The value of cooperation is placed the highest in the world, which shows we aspire to having a virtuous mind. We can attain these truths of virtue very carefully through dedication to wisdom, devotion to God, contemplation on ethics, and strength in battle.

When you look through the filter of your mind, you will always see that there is a watcher of the thoughts present. So, you can focus on your thoughts very carefully and realize which thoughts are from the programmer and which thoughts are from the virtuous mind. This mind that we aspire to be realized is containable in our lives. It doesn't take us long to change our focus, especially when we have the power within us to do so. We can then spend more time on the things that really matter in our lives, like our families, spirituality, education, and hopes and dreams for the future. So, you have to be prepared for seeing the light even greater. Your journey is far from complete; so, focus on the present. Live in the moment.

The Fourth Way of The Wise: Know Thyself

The fourth way of the wise is know thyself. In every situation, know thyself. Wisdom is shining a light in the darkness. The reflection that you find within yourself is true. To take an example of the case of human patterning that Plato spoke about, there are constantly labels being put on us that are negative, but when we know our true selves as pure, unconditional love, we will be exempt from these labels, and the mental poison will not sully us. The truth of who we are remains pure because we know our Being is unaffected and uninvolved with human patterning. If you do not know yourself, you will unconsciously identify with the label, such as ugly, stupid, incompetent, and a loser, and try to fight the battle against the ego, which will put up defenses and get angry, instead of knowing the true self which can show you your true identity once you have chosen to know you are that. Without the true self, you will allow the mental poison into your soul and your soul will be sullied, tarnished, and defiled. You will be back in Hell. The only way out of

Hell is to know yourself. Knowing thyself will give you the truth that there is a reality worth fighting for. When we know ourselves, we can find the truth to free us. The fundamental problem is self-ignorance; so, the solution is self-knowledge. Know yourself. That gives you the power to live in truth, speak the truth and act from the truth. We would be able to become one with God if we just followed this one way of the wise, for the quest would show us our kinship with the divine. We would find Heaven on Earth and get out of Hell, where we are trapped by the illusion of incompleteness, imperfection, emptiness, frailty, death, and limitation. In this Hell, we remain ignorant about ourselves. We tell ourselves lies and we live with those lies. Your journey involves going deep.

The effort of knowing yourself is the effort to attain spiritual wisdom.

The words "Know Thyself" were carved into the stone at the entrance to the temple of Apollo at Delphi, Greece.[22] What was here in the times of the ancient wisdom can be recovered. This way of the wise is held in common by almost every world religion. In John 9:25 in Christianity, it says, "He then answered, 'Whether He is a sinner, I do not know; one thing I do know, that though I was blind, now I see.'" It is an Eastern wisdom tradition to know yourself. In Confucianism, verse IV.B.14, Mencius said, "A gentleman steeps himself in the way because he wishes to find it in himself." The mightiest

---

[22] *Prot.* 343b.

warrior conquers himself, according to Confucius. In the Garland Sutra verse 36 in Buddhism, it says, "I should be a lamp for the world." This is so that you can look within your heart to understand the Dhamma within yourself.

In the Bhagavad Gita 4.37-38, in Hinduism, it says, "As the heat of a fire reduces wood to ashes, the fire of knowledge burns to ashes all karma. Nothing in this world purifies like spiritual wisdom. It is the perfection achieved in time through the path of yoga, the path which leads to the Self within." In Native Spirituality, Black Elk says, "At the center of the universe dwells the Great Spirit. And that center is really everywhere. It is within each of us." Lao Tzu, in Taoism, expresses this way as such: "Knowing others is wisdom; knowing yourself is true wisdom. Mastering others requires force; mastering yourself is true power." In Unitarianism, it says, "Wisdom, fundamentally, is knowing who you are, where you are, and what you're trying to do or be."[23]

The journey of Heaven on Earth can be made possible with wisdom.

Here we have discovered the way of self-knowledge is key. We are already getting a clear picture of the fundamental problem, so we can begin working out the solution, which comes from asking the right questions.

What is the self? That is the next big question to ask yourself. The self is the locus of thoughts, emotions, feelings, dreams, beliefs, and other mental patterns that are contained within a space of awareness in which there

---

[23] https://www.uua.org/worship/words/quote/knowing-who-you-are

is a unity within that allows you to apprehend, know, and understand through sensory experiences the world around you and grasp yourself as existing as two multiplicities, the higher and lower, or the true and false self, through introspection. The false self, we have been reminded, is the seat of complaining, to the effect of there being a worsening in our inquiry. Resentment is another one of these core aspects of ourselves and it fills us with an evil mind. When we react to something, we start the ego's domination, and it fills us with a personal grievance. Here you must know thyself to overcome the ego.

There are two selves in every person, the false self and the true self, and they reflect that there are two worlds in the person, a world of appearances that ties the false self to the illusion of imperfection, incompleteness, and emptiness, and a world of truth that reveals the true self is pure, perfect, full, whole, and complete, and unaffected by the world of pain and suffering and uninvolved in the ways of the world. The true self is unconditioned by all other things, while the false self is conditioned by the world. There are two creations in your mind when it comes to life, and you have found that the eternal Creation is endless. You can rest assured that Being is also endless. The true and false self are like this. The false self is always moving to and from an object of awareness, a pleasure, or a clinging thought, running away, and it won't stay in the same place. It has been given the name "'monkey mind".' The true self keeps the mind steady and remains constant even as the waves of emotions come. Your life can be healed by knowing that there is a true self. It is all in the mind's ability to know itself and say, "I am the *suchness*." This is part of the enlightenment of the ways of the wise, although very few go the whole way.

The effort to know yourself will be won.

The two identities of the false and true self reveal two fundamental ways of Being in the world. The deepest contemplation one can make concerns what it means to be human. The true self philosophy reveals that human nature is fundamentally good and has a relationship that is God-centered, while the false self system reveals that relationships are primarily human-centered. Because of deception, a veil of ignorance covers the mind, and sin is introduced from this sense of separation from others, and from Creation. Separation is the essence of the false self. Sin causes a disconnection from God and your deepest Being. Purification washes away the sin. With Being, there is no separation; only a love that purifies you through caring, pleasantness, and life. Separation is the cause of fear, violence, and suffering. Fear enters into your life when you forget your Being, and joy, happiness, and love exit. The false self is a fearful self. By uprooting the cause of suffering, the violence can end. When you discover the true self, you realize that you are not separate, but your spirit is unified with wisdom, and this unity is the foundation of ultimate reality, goodness, beauty, and love. Oneness is the true center of ourselves. How can your life get any bigger than this?

Don't be dismayed. Your effort to discover the truth about yourself will take you into an area of self-knowledge, and this is the highest form of wisdom.

Here the sign of life is wisdom.

Empty yourself of the desires of the body and fill yourself with the desires of your heart. You are not the self that desires. You are not the self that wants things. You are not the self that likes or dislikes. You are not the self that is impassioned or in pain. You are not the self that is consumed by cravings. You are not the self that has a burning attachment to sense pleasures. You are not the self that chases after these pleasures and craves for them. You are not the self influenced by worldly concerns. Then, what self am I? Listen to the wisdom of the Masters. They tell you that you are the self that is eternal, immortal, and blissful. You only needed to be reminded. You heart is free. Be skilled in the self-examination of your thoughts, and you will experience spiritual progress and the essential teaching of the Masters will last longer. When you recollect these things of yourself, your mind is free from hatred, greed, and delusion and your heart is pure. At this time, you are lifted to the higher realms of reality. The light that you perceive in your mind is the light that doesn't die. This is called Being. Love is also the journey within.

When you know yourself, you can find the truth about yourself in every situation. For example, if you hear that you are depleted of energy, you can say, "My true self is limitless." You can always talk to yourself when you find you have a true self and say the correct thing. The error of the false judgement has no hold on you. The false judgement is why suffering happens. We judge ourselves as imperfect, impure, unwise, limited, incomplete, empty, and lacking wholeness, and we compare ourselves to others that we perceive are greater than our own self, when in reality, your Being is divine. We mirror the divine each time we practice the ways of the wise. You can find out why you are doing the things you are doing when you know yourself. You can transcend the outside world and say, "I will not be confined by the world." When you assert, "I am here," you will be making a cosmic assertion. You won't be left in the dust when you are considered by the cosmos.

The sacred texts in world religions also point to there being an original nature or true form that is knowable. In the Holy Bible in Luke 17:20-21, in Christianity, it says, "The kingdom of God is within you." The search for meaning belongs to the kingdom within. In Psalm 139, it describes this original nature in Judaism: "I praise you, for I am fearfully and wonderfully made. Wonderful are your works; my soul knows it very well. My frame was not hidden from you, when I was being made in secret, intricately woven in the depths of the earth. Your eyes saw my unformed substance; in your book were written, every one of them, the days that were formed for me, when as yet there was none of them." In Jainism, it says, "Therefore he who aims at Nirvana must not say, 'I love this, this is mine.' Then he can very well be devoted to his own true self which is Siddha or the perfect one. Through that same self-realization he will attain Nirvana."[24] It is the way of the Masters to know they have a true self. It is what one can find in their original

---

[24] Acarya Kundakunda's Pancastikaya-sara, Kundakunda, Pancastikaya 170, p. 135.

nature. This original nature is the beginning and the end. It is who you came on this planet to be, when you have forgotten all the falsities of the world. Hinduism says in the Chandogya Upanishad verse 6.8.7, "That which is the finest essence — this whole world has that as its soul. That is Reality. That is the Self (Atman). That art thou." In the Baha'i faith, it says, "The Purpose of the one true God, exalted be His glory, in revealing Himself unto men, is to lay bare those gems that lie hidden within the mine of their true and inmost selves."[25] In Buddhism it says, "For him who... knows his own mind and sees intuitively his own nature, he is a Hero, a Teacher of gods and men, a Buddha."[26] What you will find when you look within is Buddha Nature, which gives one the power to triumph over all barriers, and even over death itself. Huang-po describes the Buddha nature: "That which is before you, is it, in all its fullness, utterly complete. There is naught beside. Even if you go through all the stages of a Bodhisattva's progress towards Buddhahood, one by one; when at a single flash, you attain a full realization, you will only be realizing the Buddha Nature which has been with you all the time, and by all the foregoing stages you will have added to it nothing at all."[27] You can discover wisdom when you discover your Being. You can be in your original nature when you have found the way to know yourself. Love can abound in the original

[25] Beyond Tolerance, Religion and Global Community, by Allen McKiel, Gleanings from the Writings of Baha'u'llah 132.
[26] Sutra of HuNeng, http://www.unification.net/ws/theme022.htm
[27] Zen Sourcebook, Traditional Documents from China, Korea, and Japan, edited by Stephen Adiss, Stanley Lombardo,

nature. You can learn to live with higher wisdom, and feel eternality.

What you have found when you uncover yourself like a buried treasure is that you are unlike other people. This may make it seem as if you don't belong, but the truth is that your belongingness is in the eternal realms of reality. This is also where you can find your home. Yet there is an original nature in all beings. It is the truth of who they are. When you endeavor to know yourself and go the way of the wise, we can find that it is being set free by way of its being without conditions in the human consciousness. We find that ego patterns place conditions on the self, and this is what gives them drama in their life story. We don't know ourselves, and that's why we obey the human patterning. When we have this awareness, we will understand. When we practice love without conditions for both our self and others, we are on the path to enlightenment, but when we love with conditions, we are again entrapped in Hell. The goal is to get out of Hell.

When Socrates strived to know himself, he discovered something very powerful. The famous question, "Who is the wisest of all men?" was asked to the Oracle of Delphi in Athens. Now the Pythia replied that there was no one wiser than Socrates. It said, "This one of you, O human beings, is wisest, who, like Socrates, recognizes that he is in truth of no account in respect to wisdom."[28] This prompted Socrates to do the work and to search for the truth. He said, "I am still even

---

[28] Apol. 23a.

now going about searching and investigating at the god's behest anyone, whether citizen or foreigner, who I think is wise: and when he does not seem so to me, I give aid to the god and show that he is not wise."[29] He went to those that had a reputation for wisdom, when he realized "I thought to myself, 'I am wiser than this man; for neither of us really knows anything fine and good, but this man thinks he knows something when he does not, whereas I, as I do not know anything, do not think I do either. I seem, then, in just this little thing to be wiser than this man at any rate, that what I do not know I do not think I know either.' "[30] Socrates performed great labors in order to prove that the Oracle was irrefutable. He then described how he went to the public men and to the poets, yet he found again that what they composed was not by wisdom, but by nature, and because they were inspired, like the prophets and givers of oracles; for these also say many fine things, but know none of the things they say. They thought that they were wise on account of their poetry, but they were not. So, Socrates went away from them also thinking he was superior to them. Then Socrates went to the hand-workers. He was conscious that he knew practically nothing, and he knew he should find that they knew many fine things. He said how the good artisans also seemed to him to have the same failings as the poets; because of practicing art well, each one thought he was wise in the other most important matters, and this folly of theirs obscured their wisdom.

---

[29] Apol. 23a.
[30] Apol. 21d.

So he asked himself on behalf of the Oracle whether he should prefer to be as he is, neither wise in their wisdom nor foolish in their folly, or to be in both respects as they are.

He said, "It was better for me to be as I am."[31] Socrates did what was necessary to know the truth. He called nothing his own and was truly wise. He had few wants. He did the work throughout his life to prove the Oracle's truth, and to know, without doubt and error, his true self. Be aware when you say, "I know", that you really do not know. Be wise. It will make your life accountable.

Should you become lost, place within your heart this motto, Know yourself, for it is known that this motto has power within. The way that you were going all leads to this final key. There is a truth within yourself that has the knowledge to be revealed. There is something that can be known from your inquiry into truth. Don't let the external self, show you that your truth is an illusion. Then you would come to disbelieve what was meant for you to believe. The opportunity to find this greatness is not to be missed. There are turns in every life that can lead you astray, and that will be the cause of self-ignorance. But with the memory of this inscription, you can go out of the dark. Self-knowledge cannot be taught. It has to be returned to you. This key is the one that holds all the others together. Don't lose the importance of it.

---

[31] Apol. 22d.

Knowledge leads to enlightenment. Waking up is turning the hands of time.

It is implied within the motto to know yourself that all knowledge is within. You need only draw out the wisdom using the method of questioning and answering as you would draw out the water from a well. All knowledge is inborn. It is already there within the mind of the knower. You must therefore search within to know yourself and allow the teacher to draw out the truth through philosophy. Just be open. The power of human recollection gives you access to this knowledge. The world that you thought was part of you is not alive when you consider the truth. There is a soul within you that had a vision of the truth before being given this body. The problem is that human patterning has imprinted the soul with lies, delusions and falsities, and we have come to believe in the appearances of truth, rather than truth. A seed has been planted in your mind to know that you have a real Being.

You know that you can find the power within you for knowledge. You can learn the knowledge in the sacred texts. Here the wisdom is organized for you to go deeply into the texts. When there is a concern for self-knowledge, you can always say, "I found myself here." The places that you find yourself are pure evidence of there being a Way. The world that you seek to learn knowledge from is not the way. The thoughts that you think are open to objectification so that you can look at each thought and say, "I am not the thought." You can separate yourself from each thought and examine it, taking it apart and considering whether it reflects your truth. These thoughts have been powerful in your life because they have defined a sense of self. So, you find that these thoughts are self-evidently true for being you. Instead, they have been very deeply imprinted in your life. If they do not reflect the true self, then the thoughts are lies, delusions, and falsities about yourself. You can find within yourself an inner judge, and this part of your self can judge the world, others, and yourself, but many things offend the inner judge; so, we must be careful and proceed only according to the truth. The truth is that each time we judge, we create a sense of separation between ourselves and others, and we become separate from God. We must only let the inner judge lead our thoughts with reason. We feel a sense of separation because we do not accept other people for being themselves fully and we reject their beliefs. How many times have you said, "I hate myself" or "I hate that person"? We become separate from God when we judge others because we have gone against our moral sense. We often blame people for something they have done, but this is only spreading mental poisons. We are programmed to make automatic judgements about other people's behavior, but when we stop and look at our thoughts, observe them and become aware of them, we can stop the judgement and feel there is unity again. Ultimately judgements are a failure to see reality for what it is and we fail to see the truth of God. To know yourself, you will succeed.

The soul possessed by God is evidence of a pure heart. This is called God-in-me. God lives in you. You may truly say, "God in me is my health right now," and "God in me is my strength; I overflow with vitality."

There is a truth that lives within you forever. It is the divine indwelling presence of God that the noble disciple aspires to in the search to know yourself. You are neither god, nor human, but both. Know yourself is the greatest thing you can recover in your thought of being complete.

We can stop judging when we stop blaming other people for not meeting our standards, or for failing to see something clearly, and when we are mindful about our thoughts. When we start to see that God is everything and everything is God, and repeat this as a mantra, we can start to see the basic goodness in all things. This will stop the human patterning of judgmental spirit and heal our hearts. We turn off judgmental spirit when we affirm the truth about ourselves. The truth will set you free. This makes us feel good about ourselves, so we practice self-love instead of self-hate, and when we love ourselves, we can follow the five ways of the wise easier. The education you receive from learning the ways of the wise helps stop judgmental spirit by making you aware of the truth of a higher reality and how to be on God's path. The love that you find within yourself when you stop judging other people is very powerful. The days are gone that you feel you could hurt another person when you identify with love.

When you take a look at the way humans interact, you will find that they are constantly self-serving. So, you are constantly thinking, speaking, and acting in ways that are not following the love of Creation. This gives us no opportunity to consider the feelings of others. We find ourselves deeper in separation. This is the cause for suffering. This separation is like a war. We find that we

178

don't have the characteristics to be closer to others, and close to God. We end up losing our heart connection. The practice of the ways of the wise has to be restarted if we lose our heart connection. The energies that you put into judging others are evil. They can usurp the fountain of youth. They can stop your love from even going to the beyond. The world will respond by going away. There are only mental disturbances that come from judgement. Most of our judgements are opinions about other people, and about ourselves. They are not truth. We have to know the truth in order to stop the judgement. Through human patterning, we learn that opinions are the normal way to express ourselves, but as we grow older, we learn that being opinionated is not right. In fact, it serves to only add pure poison into our mind and others. By taking the first step of conscious awareness, we can stop being opinionated and start focusing on truth. Only truth will stop the opinions about others and remove the patterns that have been imprinted into us since we were children. Sharing opinions has become normal. They represent the way of the outside world and how they pattern us to keep us down. Opinions keep us in the darkness, while the truth takes us into the light. The way of the prophet is to share truth, not opinions, so this is attuning you to a greater consciousness. This awareness of the prophet gives you the life that you want to enjoy. Heaven on Earth is coming up.

There are thousands of opinions that have been imprinted into our psyche over our lifetime. Opinions such as "I am always late", "I don't take my life seriously", and "I don't care as much as I should" are not self-knowledge. They do not share the fundamental truth of Being as identical to God. The truth is that you are pure, unconditional love. This means, you are pure, perfect, full, whole, and complete. This is self-knowledge. It affirms our original form and true nature. The false self is what is identified with opinions and becomes limited, based on the opinions, because it is the lower self. The true self is uninvolved and unaffected by opinions because it is the higher self.

The opinions of those around you are part of the mental chaos. They are not right to be considered as your reality; they have no soul and no life with them. The excuses and meddlesomeness are not right to behold God. Sure, as one opinion can lead to you one outside thing, and another opinion to another outside thing. There is no place for truth and justice within the world of opinions. So, follow the lead away from this darkness into a world where you can believe love is real. Belief is the attainment of God. Let your belief show you how the spiritual *logos* can teach you about self-knowledge. Knowing yourself can only come when you allow yourself to believe that you have a real self. This is beyond doubt. Go deeper within, and then you will grasp an identity with that which is and understand yourself as pure Being. Self-development is inevitable on this path. Let this awaken you. Love is naturally indwelling in everything, and when you realize this, you will be the love that God knew was your truth. This growth is the transcendence of the external world and the entrance into the Great Mystery.

When you stop the false pleasures and bodily desires, like a true warrior, you shall truly rise up like the sun in the five ways of the wise. Life is like a hero; it transcends the waywardness of collective consciousness. But with the five ways, the war is over. In truth, you are no longer a warrior when you know yourself because there is a place allowed for you to stop the war. When you allow the philosophical part of the soul to rule your soul, you will cease being war-like. You will take off the mask and put down your weapons. You will have peace within your mind and harmony within your soul. What was once war-like will be contained by the truth of the heart of the peacemaker. The reality of war is not in the philosopher's mind because he generates love. Following the mindset of the warrior is destructive to your soul, but unconsciously we think it's the way of triumph and automatically fight the entity within and other people. The warrior patterning neither benefits you nor produces any sufficient results. You can find the peace within.

In the crisis of identity, the true and false self can come into conflict because the ego does not want to die. There can even be a warring in the soul. When this happens, there is an internal conflict. We are not in harmony with our thoughts, words, and actions. What true self living teaches us can come into conflict with what we do in our social roles. We say we are one thing, but express it differently in the crisis of identity. We can be thinking in one way and acting in a different way. Have courage. Be brave. Do not give in to weakness. Resist the temptations of the false self to turn your eyes away from what is good. Follow the path of right action and you will be guided with wisdom to do the right thing in each situation. With philosophy, you will develop self-control and self-discipline and learn to act rightly, so that when the false self tries to turn your mind away from right action, the spirited part of your soul will overcome false pleasures. Drinking is a habit of the weak. The wise person will abandon self-indulgences and attain clarity of Being. Don't give up. You can develop a harmonious soul ordered by intelligence. When you learn to live harmoniously, you will find peace and joy. The way is like this: eternal, unchanging, and constant, like the true self, never wayward and disorderly, like the false self.

The light increases as truth deepens. The light responds to the truth. Becoming one with the truth is becoming one with the light. The light is the true, radiant consciousness. This is what enlightenment is; the unborn, uncreated essence that cognizes itself as pure, perfect, full, whole, and complete. You should recollect your Being like this. When you know this is your real self, by identifying with the truth rather than falsity, the delusions are eradicated, and the false self dies and you awaken. You are already there because you have the true self within you. There is nowhere to go and nothing to do. It is only a matter of identification with what is real. Then you become aware of what is, rather than remaining ignorant. When you stop identifying with what is false, your mind takes hold of the light within and shines in pristine awareness. When you stand apart from the self, analyze it, and evaluate it for what it is, you can make a shift in your mental awareness to make a distinction between the real and false self, and choose to identify with the eternal self. As it says in the Tao Te Ching verse 16, "To know the eternal is enlightenment."

The wise person will affirm, "My self doesn't die" with complete knowledge of one's immortality and divinity. The ways of the wise lead more deeply into an experience of purity of mind and create within you a humble and pure heart. When your heart is free, free from associations to the body and mind, and the ego is dropped — the "me" and "mine", you will attain bliss. See beyond the "me" and "mine" to attain enlightenment. At the same time as the soul is experiencing emptiness, it is being filled with the Great Wisdom. Do not confuse self-emptying with self-annihilating, because it is only little by little that you will say, "I am not that," as you stop identifying with the characteristics, attitudes, and qualities of the false self. This is not self-annihilating, but emptying the self.

Do we have to find God in order to find ourselves? Since the truths about God contain the most fundamental truths about ourselves, we must know God in a deep way, so it is true that once we find God, we find ourselves, but not apart from him, rather in Him. If, in knowing ourselves in God, we would know ourselves as love.

When we first attempt to discover our Being, we discover the monkey mind, which wanders all over the place. This is why it is also called the wandering mind. Choose to walk on God's path to stop the wandering mind. A wandering mind is an unhappy mind. When you feel your mind wandering out of control, you have to put your mind right. The thoughts to think of in order to stop the wandering mind are on goodness, on love, and on truth. The wise man thinks of friendship, compassion, charity and caring, and by thinking of these things he will no more want to harm a person, to lie, to steal, to be double-tongued, to drink to intoxication, to commit false witness against his neighbor, or to commit adultery, and he will learn to transcend all the evils that come from disrupted, disordered and chaotic thinking. With thoughts on goodness, love, and truth, the mind will no longer have worry, doubt, depression, anger, confusion, and feelings of condemnation. This takes concentration. When a thought of evil arises, the alert, cautious, and attentive mind will think of a good thought and begin to purify the soul with each good thought. This is called purification. It removes the defilements that come from the false self. It is what is necessary to become a good person. Leaving behind the false self for the true self is about perfection in thinking. Having the courage to think perfectly requires philosophy. Do not go into the wandering mind without bracing yourself, because you can get lost, but by holding onto what is real, you can make it through. Choose where you are going in life, because the wandering mind will try to stop you from realizing your goals. You will become frustrated and unhappy when the wandering mind controls your direction. Don't get distraught when you feel the ego take over your life. Look to the truth, now and always.

Perfection cannot be taken from the real self because it is always at peace. What it knows is truth. This alone can lead to enlightenment because you are constantly affirming the life that God said is part of His. Can you not tell your real self that it is loved? Don't go back into the falsity that the ego says is you. We are constantly trying to affirm the knowledge of what is good, so that you can be life-affirming, and not death-affirming. Something showed you the way: it was truth. The world is eager to tie you down; so, you have to wrestle with the false self, when in reality life is always in the present. Awaken to know that it was you seeking the good. It is here, in the present. Turn away from what the world has said is important and look only to the ways of wisdom; then you will come into knowledge of what is real, and true, and attain happiness. Happiness is definitive of a well-loved person, so loving yourself is the right thing to do. You can live fully with this wisdom.

The desire for a divine reality is inside all humans. It is what drives the deep search within to know yourself as the maxim of all maxims on the sacred Path. The quest to know thyself is the desire to grasp something utterly reliable, something loyal and true, something unforgettable, indestructible, incorruptible, and pure, and something eternal and shining.

Philosophy is the means to arrive at knowing the true self. It employs a question and answer method by the teacher. By asking penetrating questions, the teacher can go beneath the surface of things that the senses perceive in order to arrive at an intellectual understanding that reveals the essence of what a thing is, including what the true self is. The true teacher does not allow the noble disciple to simply accept the truth of the appearances of things, but makes the disciple see with the eyes of the heart to perceive the truth of Being. The teacher brings the true self out of the darkness of the appearances of the false self, taking the disciple beyond the realm of sensory experience. The teacher facilitates transcendence. Happiness can be attained by the pursuit of wisdom, which means to become as like to God as possible for you to become. This is the true aim of the philosopher.

Feelings of lostness are not to be confused with not having a true self, as this was given to all human beings. So, do not be dismayed when these feelings arise.

Coming into your life will always be setbacks. These are the times you need to look deeper and more closely at what it is you are trying to discover about yourself. The journey cannot be of brokenness, but of wholesomeness. It's not just that you will repair your soul; it is that you will give it a thought in itself that "'I am here.'" Then your inner self can expand like a flower. Always there is a place for learning that supersedes the discovery because there is a lesson within your soul; so, you must come into this knowingness soon, unless the lesson will say "I have to be repeated" until you find out what you are here to realize. Know the greatest things are yet to come. Your love to know yourself is the quest for Heaven on Earth.

The true self is the way you remember how it was when you were in love. This way was not just about roses and flowers that bloom, sunrises and sunsets, thank you letters and love letters, but about a deep feeling that you had inside you that you would get when you say "'yes'" to eternal life, which is the only thing that is real. He who says "'yes'" will be set free because the resounding affirmation will give you a new sense of life.

God is the one true self behind all other selves. He is the ear behind the ears, the eye behind the eyes, the nose behind the nose, and the Divine Mind behind the mind. What is behind the mask is the life of God. In the Holy Bible in Luke 12:2, it says, "You can't keep your true self hidden forever; before long you'll be exposed. You can't hide behind a religious mask forever; sooner or later the mask will slip and your true face will be known." Never can you be moved from this life. Healing is like attuning yourself to a way that is greater than you can imagine. This attunement is drawing you nearer to the reality of His nature.

The truth within the soul is not to be tarnished. There is a new thing within the soul that is called real. That is the bigness within the soul, and it can't be reduced to nothing. The call within the heart is also part of this bigness. It can't be reduced to nothing either. It can be presented as the true self. It doesn't matter who said what to define yourself; those personalities aren't real. Then the turn within to know yourself is a turn to realize eternal life. You can't not be transformed when you are following the ways of the wise because the Masters have created a Path for you to move in the inner worlds. This kind of soul journey is never one in which you know yourself from the minds of others, but the true self is revealed by the teacher's love.

Here, your goal is to perfect the wisdom.

To find that you are, as if, in a prison is to find that you have plunged yourself there by riveting the thoughts of yourself into the body, revealing the dominance of the lower self over the higher self. The way of freedom is to separate these thoughts carefully from the truth of what is and attune yourself rightfully to what is real. Be aware of the bodily senses and know what the body is not. Knowing you have a true self is the cause of happiness and freedom. This is not from the outside or from the inside. It simply is, always. Where? Everywhere. Freedom is the most basic condition to happiness. This freedom is not just political freedom, but also freedom from mental disturbances, such as anger, hatred, jealousy, sadness, and delusion. There will be a loss of consciousness in your mind when you fill your life with these evils. These mental constructs are a product of ignorance. As long as evil remains in the heart, happiness will never result. You can never lose when you have wisdom.

The life that you had once thought to be real is not the reality that God planned for you. The reality that God planned for you is far greater; you could be living a far better life. There is knowledge, truth, goodness, beauty and abundance overflowing from His everlasting Kingdom to your soul so that you may come to know that the immeasurable greatness is there for you to receive from the grace of God. Healing is about being able to receive the gift of a new life and be grateful for all that He has done for you. Don't stop being open to this greatness. Receiving God's life is what you are trying to do so that you can be one with His life.

Be in your own truth, and you will find the cause of all life's purpose, and this will uproot the enemy called death. For knowing all life's purpose is part of beholding the greatness within so that you may come to enjoy what that greatness truly is. He who knows how to destroy the darkness will come into the light. Being set free from all suffering is in the phrase "I am." The philosopher René Descartes famously said, "I think, therefore I am," thereby affirming that he is a thinking essence and equating thinking with Being. But according to Jean-Paul Sartre's insight in philosophy, "Existence precedes essence", there is a need to affirm "I am" in order to affirm your existence as prior. Existence is awareness. Awareness is existence. These words contain both the seed and the flower of awakening. Whosoever utters those words is alive in their life, and this will free you from all external circumstances because you have declared yourself to be present.

There is no mystery within if you have Being to show you the way because whatever is within will be given to you through the eternal light. The eternal light is God. He who holds the eternal light will be given the gift of immortality. But know that it can be withheld if you remain ignorant. So, don't just tell stories, but look for the truth. When you are caught in the net of non-being or falsehood, you are hidden from yourself. The answer to this difficulty is Being or truth; then you will be found. There is no hidden Being or hiddenness in truth. Everyday life is a path, yet when you realize truth, there is an end to the journey and you can find peace and happiness within, knowing you have completed the Path and followed the way of the teacher; then you will have become as free as the sky. In this spaciousness, you will realize what it takes to know yourself and become free.

The light that you seek to become is the perfection of wisdom. Light is a form of who you are and it is the way within. Coming to know yourself is the light of truth. You will perceive that light shines, but it is really you that is shining. You exist, you shine. This means that you are knowable. Light emulates what you are within. Coming into Being is about exploding with light. Truth brings the light into your Being. When seeing the light for the first time, there is proof of an eternal Being within you. Coming into your true self is like being in the light of God. What was once hidden can be seen in the light. What you call light is like the eye that is seeing. It has the inward thought that you are here. Your evidence that you are pure light is found only in the teacher's mind. Be a disciple. You can become something that the teacher thought about, then you will be perfect, for what he thinks are in the higher realms of reality, so you would come to emulate this higher truth. The disciple is a believer. The teacher's light showed you who you are in the beginning, so his light will never go out. The light of God is where a teacher began. Should you think that you are not perfect, he will test your mind, and find the error of your ways. It's beyond advice what he will give. It's a method of inquiry into your life and the cause of things that will help you realize that you can indeed succeed on this path. The teacher can give you peace. The teacher is peace. The teacher reveals the truth within your heart and by imitating all the godlike characteristics of the teacher, you can realize the god within yourself.

The world within is not to be destroyed by a love of pride, or an obsession, or a thing of greatness. It cannot be tarnished. It is pure beyond belief. It is a treasury of unfolding truth, beauty, and goodness. Only God knows the way for you to be found. Only the Creator can grant you that there is a world within. It is a gift once you know yourself. Just allow that moment to be in yourself and then you will be self-realized. Don't go far from the truth that was given to you. Be alive in the moment. Great is what God thought of you when you were created. God's thought of yourself is perfect. Just speak from your heart, the words, "I want to know," then you will attain a single-pointed mind of concentration, with a focus on truth and justice, which is singular. Let your eye be single and your eye will be filled with light.

Did you ever think the world within was a cause of your own life? Then you could examine what the reality of that life is, and put that life into existence with your truth. You could be bearer of all that is, knowing for certain that there is a way within. The world outside can be detrimental to the world within. Welcoming you into this existence is like trying on your life for the first time.

The false self is a self-image or a projection. It is like a movie on a screen that creates a reality so that life is a dream or a show. The images are endless because the mind clings to thoughts and has attachment. They are impressions on the self that can only be erased when you discover the peace and joy of your Being. The projection of a self-image causes separation and a divided self. This is the cause of suffering, and it is an illusion. To find the true self, you must sort through the mental images of the false self and identify with the true self. The wise person will value observation and a quiet mind as the keys to dissolving the images away. Simply observe these images and continue to identify with the true self. The light of the observer is the same light as God. The light of truth will shine through the images to reveal your Being in clear light. Go beyond the mind and enter into the place of truth to become one with truth. This is transcendence. The truth is: you are one with God. To awaken, stop the projection of the myths and metaphors, the stories and roles of the false self. The universe is real. There is a real self that exists that does not have dependent existence, unlike the false self, which is dependent upon the intellect, light, and God for its life. It is the one thing that is not an illusion. Life is not a dream if you can wake up. Go forward knowing you can find the deep self.

Who knows the truth but God himself? So, knowing this is about drawing close to His mind and being open to His gift of reality. This way, you won't be left out when you see the external world for what it is, and you can come into His presence with all confidence that you will be loved. This is the reality that is given to you in a treasure box. All that you ever wanted to be is contained within. Opening up your treasure box is like traveling to a spirit world. It is a divine power. Let your soul know that you have come a long way. Then make time for your awakening each moment. Should you think that you are not worth bringing this reality to manifest, then you are lost in your ego and you need to hold onto the Path as the mirror to light up your life. Give yourself this self-knowledge; then the dreaming world will be long gone. See that you remain present for the love to take hold, for life is only happening in the present. Here the soul has the opportunity to know itself.

The five ways of the wise bring meaning into your life from the fact that it concerns truth and the revelation of truth. That itself is meaningful. When you find your true self, you will find meaning. Life is not meaningless. But what is the meaning of life? We search for the meaning of life very deeply, and the truth is that life's meaning is finding that our own finitude is not to be taken from us, for being alive is deeply meaningful itself. If you feel that you can't find any meaning, follow the Path to Freedom and Self-Mastery. Search there and do not look elsewhere. If you follow this Path, hundreds of thousands of loves will come from this search and fill the heaven and the earth.

Love was an eternal thought that you could be known by a bigger thing, and the five ways of the wise can help you find this bigness fully present in your life. What is the eternal? It is the presence of a mind of God. Coming into contact with the Divine Mind can show you that His life and your life are not separate or apart from each other. His life is put inside your heart so that you can walk the path of love by understanding the real self is what God has created from a thought that you are perfect. The moment that you understand that you are the true self, you will attain divinity, immortality, and bliss, and you will find that the pleasures you had before that were temporary and short-lived will be replaced with true pleasures as bright as the brilliant sun. Wisdom is the greatest of these pleasures.

Knowingness is not just the way of spiritual Masters, but the idea of what you came here for. The truth lives in the mind of the Masters, so you must move with them, rather than letting them move you. Breaking free is an aspect of this movement. The reality of Heaven on Earth is not being discounted. We have concluded that the mind can transcend and encompass Being. Losing touch with yourself will be repaired. Coming home will be the soul journey. Entering into God's space, which is the greatest light, will be the way so that you can unlock the truth within. Socrates discovered his existence himself by going inward. He became the light for others, that they too would shine through the darkness and arise, ascend, and awaken. This is flowing.

The healing journey with the five ways of the wise is a journey home. With each search for Being, you will come closer to your heart, where your inner voice reveals the truth of your hidden nature, causing you to delve deeper into your purpose for being here. Home is the present moment where the ego dissolves away into the infinity and bliss of your oneness with God. Practicing presence is bringing yourself to the realization that life is happening right here, and right now. Live in faith. There is a way to return home that is found by walking with the Masters who teach you the wisdom of renunciation, purification, self-emptying, and prayer. Just wake up and take notice. Overcoming the loss of the false self is not the end of the world. Love is what remains when you awaken. Something "'other'" is not what the false self is; it is a non-existent truth. If you believe something has been lost when you read your life-story, be at peace knowing that it can be found when you know your real self is pure, perfect, full, whole, and complete. There can only be this person that says, "I am that I am", and none other. It is the real self. It has infinity, eternality, indestructability and incorruptibility within the true nature. From the deep eye of truth, it has a flower of awareness. Coming into yourself is about allowing the soul to be alive. Be centered in peace and know that it is true what you have come into. When affirming "I am that I am", this means "I will be what I will be."

At the core of our belief is a mind that defines our self-identity as useless; so, in order to combat this illness within, we need make an effort to realize our function. Express your function. What your sole purpose is, is the acceptance of who you are. Coming into this knowledge is not about going outside to do something other or be something other. It's awakened within the mind of God, so you just need to become one with God; then your purpose will be given to you. What your essence is, is your truth. This truth is greater than a life story, but a story of life. How does it feel to be you? What is meaningful in your life has within it the power to awaken your purpose, beyond the patterns, belief systems, habits, and behaviors, which are not the real you. Your soul knows the way.

Often it is not only words that get in the way of reality and in the way of knowing ourselves. It is our very own egos, just as we know from the tale by Hans Christian Andersen called *The Emperor's New Clothes* in which the emperor could not see that he had no clothes, but only the little girl could see this truth. What was lost by the emperor was seen by the little child, who could see reality better than the emperor. The ego got in the way of reality. We have all been given the power to be here now, but the emperor could not live in that space of truth. He had within himself the right to cry, "These are mine", and he could see what he wanted to see better than the others could, but he did not imagine that the wisdom of the child could far surpass him. Instead of pausing and taking that wisdom into consideration, the emperor didn't believe it because he allowed his pride to get in the way of reality. What you can understand from this story is that one voice may not be as powerful as the ego's voice. This has to do with self-denial. What you are denying is the truth of the way things are. The truth was shown to the emperor, but he stubbornly disagreed. This shows that the ego has a hold on reality. Reality cannot teach you anything if you do not allow it to be valid or valuable. What reality is meant to show you is that there is a love that is being lost. What could be shown, but the world within? This is ultimately where the child's revelation could take the emperor. It's this truth, that there is a way, that even the child could perceive, that can take you into a deeper space. It is his failure to be noticing the way that causes his suffering. Noticing can lead to greater awareness. He who notices the way will be alive in the child's eyes. There was a time when the innocence of the child would supersede the ego, but with grandiose inventions, such as modern ways, we have lost sight of what the child was trying to say. Can the ego ever find its way without the child's advice?

There can only be one truth. It was this truth that the emperor failed to see. Honesty can lead to greater awareness. When you tell someone the truth, you can attune yourself to the way of the child. This has to do with becoming pure. And essentially this has to do with becoming light. What was needed at the time for the emperor to see the truth was innocence. You can congratulate yourself if you find this innocence within you. It is a great feat. What was true a long time ago for the emperor can be true once again. This way has to do with love, hope, beauty, and truth. The ultimate reality is that there is a way that can be spoken about. This way is not hidden from the masses. By saying something, you can reveal the truth. So, it is the utmost in the highest to be responsible with the language you use. So, it is this power of innocence that can be yielded to kill the enemy called egoism. Life was not made without innocence.

How can the return to innocence be done with so much evil in the world? One may question it, along with a sense of wonder. Herein lies the gift of yourself. It is that you can be trusted to find the five ways of the wise. It is here that you can even find your own truth. This truth does not deviate from the fourth way of the wise. It is consistent and it is applied to all things. You cannot forget your innocence. It is the call to remember who we are; that is why we are here. This call is ever the deeper when you hear the story of the emperor reflected into his own self, which will give him the power to remember who he is and why he is here. This is the greatness of the lost and the found. He who remembers himself can find the ways of the wise. It is not a myth of innocence if there is a way of the wise because the way of the wise shows the innocence can be recovered by knowing that you have a way within. This is the height of truth. Turning to investigate by yourself, for yourself, in yourself, is how the way of the wise begins. When you come to know what life is, you will come to say, "I am here" and this will be the child's revelation as well. Taking a lesson at hand, this lesson teaches you to be yourself fully, even in the most dire circumstances, because when you are acting from your own soul, you will find the child's eyes with you. Then you can take your life back. The ways of the wise are the way of life.

There has always been something "'out there".' Yet it is also within. The ways of the wise can be given to all people. There is something that can be aspired to. The shift into self-consciousness, as the emperor knew, is not just a process, but it can be thought of as something sacred. The five ways of the wise can be brought into your life with love because at the very core of their existence is the fact that you can be recovered. This has to do with knowing that you are true in yourself. What this amounts to is that you are here. You are not gone from your self-consciousness, but are alive to the day. The turning of the mind into a life is very powerful.

But why can't the emperor see his new clothes? The answer is that because he needed others to see him and judge his attire for him. It is exactly this state of awareness that we have to flee from. We must stop allowing others to define our own reality and instead become self-reflexive so that we can judge for ourselves what is true for us and not true for us. We must become aware of ourselves to judge for ourselves what is good and not good, what is stupid and not stupid. If we leave this up to others, we run the risk of our reality being untrue. We run the risk of living a lie. And we can see that most of our lives are sustained by the false beliefs of others. The false belief is what we have to be prepared for when we exist in spiritual blindness. Taking hold of our soul means conquering the fear that we have that others are available to judge us. There is a mirror of reality that shows the sense of lostness the emperor felt. You can look into the mirror, but you cannot change what is being reflected to you. This shows there is a way that cannot be changed, so you must change yourself.

It can never be denied that there was a way in the beginning. This beginning had to do with endless thoughts on perfection, completeness, and wholeness. When the beginning was first discovered, it was thought to be a wondrous thing, and it could never be proven wrong that there was something magical. The thought of perfection itself is the thought of God. God has given the idea of perfection to all people. What was once called perfection in the emperor's mind became the child's self, because his self was so perfect that only a child could see it. This truth of the child wanting to be perfect is in everybody's consciousness. It is the reality of life itself when it wants to take hold of the beginning. There can never be a more obvious point of beginning when a child wants his body or his mind to be perfect. This call to perfection is in the order of the way itself. Saying something is not as perfect as it was once thought to be is the cause of suffering. We have all been there. This is also the place where evil begins, because the cause cannot ever be attained in the ego's mind. So, we have to let go of what we once believed was our self, and turn to another life story, one that makes more sense to our reality. We have been given the power to move from story to story. Each one reflects an instance of our self. We were taught to reflect on ourselves by someone that we loved. There are so many stories to tell ourselves that we become lost in the movie or the drama that we are watching and playing a role in.

One can imagine there is only one way of the wise, called love. When one considers what makes things real, one refers to love. But the cause of concern is greater than this. It is about truth as well. The truth that can be known from the innocence means it still exists. So, we should not shatter the doubt within our own mind that we are onto something. This something is really special. It has to do with the consciousness of Being, not becoming. Wanting to discuss the eternal is what the Taoists were doing when they discovered something called Being. It is the essence of reality itself. One can be thought of as "here", and one can be thought of as "I Am". The male part is the dominant affirmative one, while the female part is the spatial existence. Taking the two principles together, we have the love of all Creation. This reality is God. It can be taken down particle by particle by scientists, but they will never find the beginning, which exists in the sacredness of The All. It is here that humankind has found love among people, and this will, in essence, give one the power to go forward. Taking away from the now is not possible. There is a totality in all things.

When you forget who you are, there is an awakening that you can go through. Buddha taught that you can awaken the mind, without it being fixed anywhere, but remaining in the present. This is the power to become lit up with life. It's the turning away from all evil and the coming into knowledge of your whole truth. It is something that happens to a few individuals; it is not characteristic of the whole of humanity, but when it does happen, it can depict a transformation, and a blossoming, like a flower, can occur. The flower that you perceive is one that you find within yourself if you are conscious of there being a Caregiver in the universe. Allow the transformation. In this new experience, you are who you came to be, and not something other. It is a timeless, ever-present experience of the eternal. This means that you are here for a purpose, and not here to simply die out. What you can be doing with your life is revealed in that moment. And it is something great for all people. Turning your life over to God is often what people do, and when you do turn your life over to God, you can find the truths of reality, ever more clear. There is a time for all people to awaken, not just the rare individual. God placed the flower in you for wisdom.

Knowing ourselves is the right thing to do.

The Fifth Way of The Wise:
Focus on Achievements, Not Money

The fifth way of the wise is to focus on achievements, not money. Life is transforming very fast when you consider this as your wisdom. It has the effect of transforming your action in your life. It can set you free on a number of levels. Focus on achievements, not money. Keep in mind these achievements may not be worth it every time, but they will give you the power to succeed. Achievements in life cannot come and go, because they are always associated with this one big opportunity. When it says you have the power to achieve, this means you can complete something for your self-consciousness. So, this means that you can acquire a new talent or a new skill and build upon your character. The greatest character you can have is that of wisdom. When you feel that you can achieve greatness, you cannot let money get in the way of attaining something that is beyond wealth. The accumulation of wealth is catastrophic in the West. Comfort destroys the welfare of society. When you focus on achievements, not money, you can rise up in your soul and say, "I have acquired this," without having been made worthy of it. This is the true fulfillment of a great person. If you have acquired your aptitude for wisdom, this is not something that has a space of money. It is something you do purely out of the love for learning. Love will take you there. Your soul is the priority, and your life is this truth, so your life has to also be the priority. Greatness is what you will accomplish. Your journey involves this way.

There are so many achievements that the human being hopes to attain, from accelerating in his mind, to learning a language, from traveling the world, to making the biggest difference possible, to building a dream, from raising a family, to going to college. All these are built on something that money doesn't give you. They are built on the personal ability to see the truth of who you are. The achiever is greater than the average person. It goes into his life that he has achieved what money cannot do for him. There is a powerful moment in the achiever's life where he says, "I can make it." This truth can be your true story of spiritual victory. The accreditation that the achiever can find in himself is about winning. Life is won with wisdom.

You can be greater than you are. Don't look to the existence of a hero forever, but affirm your own heroism. Regardless of whether you fail or succeed at the task, continue to always focus on the achievement, not money. There are many achievements we had since being a child, and all of them came with reward or punishment. We would often succeed when we tried our hardest, and fail when we put the least amount of effort into the goal. The accomplishments were greater than life. You can succeed if you put your mind to it. That's what we would often hear. The chance of achieving is greater when you put your mind to it. There is a will within all people. Keep up with your soul journey steadily.

A Heaven-sent purpose is in the means to achieve.

The way to focus on achievements, not money, is advocated by major world religions. They talk about the renunciation of wealth as the way of the wise, and victory as the way of achievement. In Matthew 6:24 in Christianity it says, "No one can serve two Masters; for either he will hate the one and love the other, or he will be devoted to the one and despise the other. You cannot serve God and mammon." In Taoism, Chuang Tzu says in verse 29 of the Tao Te Ching, "Do not chase after riches, do not risk your life for success, or you will let slip the Heaven within you." In the Qur'an chapter 104, 1-3 in Islam it says, "Woe is he . . . who has gathered riches and counted them over, thinking his riches have made him immortal!" In Dhammapada verse 355 Buddha says, "Riches ruin the foolish, but not those in quest of the Beyond. Through craving for riches, the ignorant man ruins himself as he does others." These world religions teach you the heart of focusing on achievements, not money. Before you know it, the achievement can be real in your mind. It is the truth of the world religions.

The power to achieve is amazing in humankind. We have achieved the greatest feats, such as the creation of computers, airplanes, cars, and many other things, yet we are not aware of it. With awareness, our life will change completely.

Be prepared. Life brings many changes.

Renunciation means letting go of our hold on money. Let go. Do not become attached to anything. Worldly things can have a hold on you, and you need to let go of them by practicing detachment. It takes courage to let go. Use the spirit of courage to let go of all bodily desires, attachments, and pleasures. With the path of letting go, you will cultivate your soul, return to your heart, and become temperate. Take courage to let go so you can freely live and freely love. Go all the way; leave everything behind, including the external "I". There remains only the real "I" that observes through the muddied waters of the false "I". What do you have to let go of to find peace right now? When you focus on achievements, not money, you create your own individual Heaven, and when you do not focus on achievement, but money, you create your own Hell.

There is a built-in human need for wanting, because it is part of the program. We feel there is a truth in the sense of ownership to the things that we want. This makes us feel envious and greedy. We are always wanting more, as if the suffering will be removed by the replenishment of our ownership. But on the contrary, this incessant need to want what isn't yours restores the entity's power over your heart and controls you. So, you lose your power. So, we need to be bold. You need to heal the wounds at the core self. The trouble with always wanting more is that you feel the ego patterns. Lust, envy, greed, are traceable in the history of humankind to be demonstrative of the evil entity. So, stopping the talking within your mind is purposeful. The Path to Freedom and Self-Mastery in the conclusion is fueled by the end of the ego. Take heart; find wisdom to be the best way.

When we hear about the renunciation of wealth, we hear about losing all our opportunity, but this is not true. In effect, the wealth that you can attain from an achievement is far greater. We learned in the sacred texts that the dominant idea is to withdraw from the idea of money. This is so that we can be set free and purified within. Love is not participating in the wealth at all. Being confused is not unlike the state of disorder that comes from money-loving. It is not that we have become absent-minded to wealth, as it is still important to run our lives with it. This is so that we can live happier and healthier. The first way of the wise taught you to renounce selfishness and achieve a greater feeling in your life through compassionate actions; so, you can see how important this power of renunciation is. We often have to lose the whole foundation of money until we realize that the face-value of the money is not the face-value that turns to know us. The achievement within us is far greater.

There is a traditional Zen Buddhist anecdote that says: Yang-shan asked a monk, "Where have you come from?"

The monk said, "Lu Mountain."

Then Yang-shan asked, "Did you go to the Five Elders Peak?"

The monk said, "I didn't visit there."

Yang-shan said, "Then you didn't go to the mountain at all."[32]

The mountain represented something greater for Yang-shan, clearly. This had to do with the number five. He was not at peace within having gone there, without having achieved the greatest climb. Even though the mountain was right in front of his eyes, the monk missed this accomplishment, only then to receive compassion from Yang-shan concerning his journey. This may have been overdoing the quest to succeed, and his energy may have become depleted if he had tried. It would have taken longer for the monk to accomplish his goal, but the reward he would have got was not comparable to money. Heaven on Earth is the paradise you hope to attain.

The humiliation within your mind can be set free by the research that proves wisdom is the best medicine for your soul. We often feel depression when we miss an achievement. Take heart. Life on planet Earth is not a waste. Your love for wisdom will lead you to a bright future.

You often heard that you are brilliant, powerful, intelligent, competent, and a winner when you accomplish a goal and become an achiever, while if you failed to achieve, you would often hear that you are not intelligent, an underachiever, stupid, and a loser. The latter is probably what the monk was feeling. The monk may even say "I am not strong enough" or "I am not talented enough to achieve", but that is not true. He found

---

[32] 365 Spirit: A Daily Journey for your Soul, by Aaron Zerah.

self-doubt within his soul that the five ways shed light on, but the truth is that he had the spirit within him to achieve. To be happy, the monk must face this demon of doubt. When we succeed, we are praised and feel joy, triumph, and a sense of being unstoppable. When we fail, we often have frustrations, self-judgement, guilt, shame, and regret. Don't lose out on the opportunity of a lifetime.

The times may be hard for you to focus on, but don't give up. Just focus on achievements, not money. This will organize your life for healing. There is no way you can judge yourself if you always focus on achievements, not money. In the absence of self-judgement, you will not suffer from the afflictions that come from self-judgement, like guilt, blame, shame, regret, loss, despair, and self-punishment. By always staying focused on achievements, not money, you will stop the association to the illusion and you will live your life profoundly. You're going to be useful, valuable, and dynamic. Your life will be productive because the world will receive your life as generously as you give it.

When you focus on achievements, not money, you will focus on action, and be rewarded for your action. This action has to do with your soul being made to live courageously. Just do it. Focus on achievement, not money. We can have millions of ideas, but if we don't take the action, we don't manifest those ideas. The monk needed to believe this in order to be alive. This action alone is the cause for happiness. Doing this action will set the monk's life right so that there is no loss of opportunity. Completion is without reward. It is solely in the moment of saying "I did it" that it is empowering.

When you take action for the sake of taking action so that the achievement is an end in itself, not a means to an end, this will lead to finding pure enjoyment in everything you do. When all the pain subsides and the sense of separation goes, there is the experience of joy upon remembering the beauty that is within. Joy is the moment of awakening. It is the transcendence of suffering and of all evils. Joy is the resonance within of the body being set free. Go within and listen to your body to realize that it is not part of who you are. It is effortless to feel joy, which is what you attain when you lose the evils of the false self.

We often wonder, what is happiness? True happiness is a way of being in the world that makes a triumphant association to something that is valued concerning human connection, to something significant, to something that your eye can behold that reveals that the pleasantry of humankind is there to love, and to something that is greater than ourselves. This is the release of suffering. Drugs don't lead to happiness. There are many values related to achievements that one can value to attain happiness, such as completion, risk-taking, power, challenge, discovery, thrill, status, and ambition. If the monk had valued these values and focused on these inner values, he could have found that completing the climb would have led to happiness. These are the values that he needed to achieve.

There is something to say about values. They have within the mind the power to inspire. So, what was missing in the monk's life was the ability to value the values associated with the achievement. You always need a value to go forward in life. It's as if the value is the way itself. The measure of happiness is due to the power of the value. These values are the sole cause for our actions. They propel us into a greater state of Being where we can find our life to be without limit. Holding onto a value is like holding onto a truth. It is this powerful to have a value. You cannot lose when you have a value. The reward will be happiness itself. This is an end in itself. When the monk lives for the values, he can live for the dream of happiness.

Values do not come and go. They are the eternal mindset of the Savior. Blessed is he who has values of the same. Then they can be self-realized and he can learn the ways of the wise. He who values the straight path affirms the values of alertness, observance, and patience as the means of liberation through the practice of philosophy. Philosophy is not enough. It takes practice to achieve your goal. Practice makes the Master. Be cautious. And pay attention. The straight path is like a government in Heaven that is founded with values. Let these values measure the performance of all that you do, and you will find your Being without clinging to the thoughts, habits, beliefs, and patterns that arise from the false self to ruin and spoil the soul. What can ruin and spoil the soul is a valueless existence. He who has values has strength to go into the world within to conquer each mental disturbance.

Sometimes risk-taking is all that matters because you have placed your time to conquer the world and yourself. This is the element of Jesus, and it is the element of the Great Buddha. Both were met with severe conditions and reactions, but they took the risk that they could teach the world. They believed risking it all could lead to the end of suffering. This was their promise to humankind as well. Love would not be lost in their risk. There is nothing that can take the right to be wise away from you. It is inherent in the way of humanity to follow your right.

You can only be your true self when you focus on achievements, not money. The monk needed to take the risk to be himself fully, instead of denying this truth to himself to become greater than he realized. He needed to express his own true self by focusing on the achievement that Yang-shan showed to him. This is what we all need to do: express our true selves. In the currency of life, there are downfalls that take you into a spiral where nothing seems significant; so, you need wisdom to release the spell and enable you to behold the Tree of Life. You have come here for no other reason than to affirm your truth. What we often do is punish ourselves when we fail to affirm our truth, but self-punishment is only going to cause more suffering. The fifth way can release you from the spell that we are under from human patterning, which imprints our soul with the goals associated with our career and teaches us that the reward is money. These imprints can be removed by the new program that gives us a power to know ourselves greater than the human patterning. This will set us free.

When you love yourself, follow your spirit. Most people do not take action without the promise of money. That is why they do not achieve. Taking the way of the monk as the example, we find there are many occasions when we fail to achieve. When we make a promise to ourselves to do something, but if there is no money being given to us, we often do not perform the action. Something in our lives takes us away from the achievement, whether it be depletion of energy, lack of interest, lack of valuing our values, lack of knowledge, lack of time, but most times, we do not focus on achievements because there is no money as the reward. When we think about work, we are conditioned to believing that we must be paid for our achievements. We think that is the way, to be paid. But so many times we stop the clock and we say, "I'm going home to do something for myself." This is the way of the achiever. He doesn't care that the clock that he stopped isn't giving him money. This is a cause for living your life to the fullest. We like ourselves when we achieve and don't like ourselves when we fail to achieve. The achiever needs to be more conscious that he is acting for a purpose. That purpose is character, sometimes even called the human spirit. The spirit that moves within us moves for the mind that governs achievement. What Yang-shan thought he was doing was moving the spirit in the monk. The spirit in all people can be moved by greatness and the life will become great.

Achievement refines our character and builds on our character. We develop virtues from achievement, like courage, temperance, honor, respect, authenticity, excellence, patience, integrity, and commitment, and wisdom is the chief among them. This quest for achievement is the way of the virtuous mind. We can achieve virtue in our character simply by avoiding the pains that come with a vice, like stubbornness. The virtuous mind is the reward that can also come from focusing on achievements, not money. This way of the wise is very challenging, but when you rise to the challenge, you will be set free. When you focus on achievements, not money, you will learn to accept yourself. Becoming aware of your mistakes is the key. The monk had to be aware that he made a mistake in his journey to conquer himself, according to Yang-shan. This mistake was pointed out to him so that he could try again and not fail. The compassion from Yang-shan is what we all need when we are trying to achieve to see where our failures are, and our challenges. The compassion from Yang-shan gave the monk his awareness. Often, we fail to achieve because of lack of awareness. He needed to see the truth from Yang-shan. Compassion increases our awareness. This is the power of love. It was love that brought the monk up the mountain, so it was love that was trying to encourage him to go forward. Love is the greatest thing the achiever can find in himself. Focus on achievements, not money, because you want to do the action, not because you have to do the action or because you are trying to please other people, but so that you will be real in the moment. This will give you power of authenticity. If the monk took action because he had to, there is no way that he would achieve with the power of authenticity. He would fail also to have the value of truth. This is what Yang-shan said was possible even for the monk. He wanted to become a greater person, and Yang-shan saw that truth within him.

Taking action is the way of happiness, the way of fully being yourself. When we fail to act, like the monk, we fail to live our lives fully and we deny our true selves from experiencing self-expression and self-development. Yang-shan wanted the monk to be himself fully, which is the power of true self living, without denial of the truth that he knew was possible to find within the monk. You can find the power of Being in the path to the mountain. It would lead to the fullness of his truth. Taking action leads to results. Inaction leads to despair, hating yourself, and an unwholesome state of mind. Awareness is key.

There is a Chinese proverb that says, "Pearls don't lie on the seashore. If you want one, you must dive for it." The journey is worth pursuing because there is a treasure that is worth finding. You can find the hidden treasure. How can we reveal that which is hidden? The bud is revealed when the flower blooms, so too, the light within awakens when the heart blooms. Just try with all your heart, and the light will awaken. Inside the Path, there is a blooming that you can be conscious of understanding. The way will be the seed within you to give you the light you desire. The treasures that we look for are often found in our values. The greatest treasures are wisdom, compassion, and harmony. Be wise in your thoughts and you will return to God; have compassion with all people and all creatures, and find harmony in friendships and with enemies. This is like saying, it is worth coming out of Plato's cave to pursue the greatest things in life and to discover the greatest truths. Conquering yourself is the greatest achievement, for you will find that in the conquering, there is no conqueror, and that itself is the realization of true happiness. Constant abiding in the present moment will take you to this happiness.

Coming into complacency, turns the will of the mind from hard-heartedness to opportunity.

Sometimes in our lives, we miss the biggest opportunity and cannot go back to undo what was lost. When you lack something, you feel the inner depravity more powerfully when you turn your life off. We have to stay present and accept the lessons in life and remember to focus on achievements, not money. There can never be another mountain like the one called the present. This is the mountain of the greatest spiritual journey. Look to the great one called Life itself.

A mountain is a symbol for a spiritual journey. The mountain gives you the opportunity to be here now. Do not miss this opportunity to complete the achievement to know the ways of the wise. Focusing on achievements, not money, is the power to express your dream and be true to yourself. This is the way of life, not the way of death. We often feel as if we have found the way of life in the spiritual climb of a mountain, so this is true in the very real sense of the word, that we have an achievement to master. This is the climb of the way that brings us back into the sacredness of the wise. He who knows the way will find the spiritual climb true for him. Then the way can be materialized in your achievement. This way is the mind attuning itself to life. Yang-shan knew the way. Life is only in the present moment. When you let go of the idea of making money and focus on achievements, there is a power that you can find in the way that will light up the eye of truth with care because the way is all about life. Thinking you have failed is not right in any culture, so it is not right to think that you have failed. The way things are set up in society is that you will win at some things and you will lose at other things.

There is achievement that can be had in the world. Life has brought many challenges in the way. The spiritual mountain that people face at least once in their lives can be overcome. This fills your energy body with life and it gives it a sense of direction. This is the reason for achievement: that you can finish the climb in a very real spiritual sense. Wisdom is the tool needed to climb the mountain.

With this realization, you can go forward with the five ways of the wise, as if climbing a mountain. You can continue your search, knowing it is perfectly ordered in length, in width, in height, and in depth. Do not give up in your quest for truth. When you are tired and ready to give up in confusion, frustration, despair, and emptiness, find the energy, power, and the enthusiasm within yourself to go forward in your search. Although there are challenges and obstacles while climbing up the spiritual mountain, be comforted in knowing that the way is just as long as it should be. It is as if it is divinely governed by a perfect path in Heaven, and every step is perfect and each road is an opportunity to take you home. Follow the will of God. Don't turn back now. You are close to the Path of Freedom and Self-Mastery.

The truth of your love for philosophy starts your mind in an effort to know the greatest wisdom.

Coming to grips with knowing the truth of life is best done through wisdom.

The achievements of the achiever are not money-based. So, in effect, you can be set free from the hold of the world. The world is always teaching us to think about money. It is the cause of all the human programs that make the ego patterns in the psyche even deeper. These world religions are testifying to the wisdom of focusing on your achievements, not money. The love that can be found in the achiever is present because he knew something greater than other people.

Love is life unfolding through you.

When you defy all odds and succeed, you have placed a mark against the enemy. It is very likely he cannot touch you in any situation ever again. You have challenged the greatest foes when you make an achievement. Your power will be retained. Looking back into your life, you will find that all the worldly patterns within the patterning of humankind will be destroyed when you have one achievement. You have overcome the world. This way of the wise is the way to challenge even the destroyer. He had tried to take your life from you, but with a new program in your consciousness, you can overcome even his trials and tribulations.

The other ways of the wise depend on this fifth way to be successful. You have to achieve at the five ways of the wise. You will not always be able to follow the Golden Rule, listen with your heart, focus on the present, or know yourself until you make the fifth way of the wise a habit. Then your power to achieve these other ways will also become habitual. You will overcome. Learning to become great is embedded in all the ways. You will not feel defeat when you make the ways of the wise a habit. Just believe and you will achieve. The love that you have for the wisdom will give you triumph. When you forget these ways, you will feel defeat, but you have to write them down and make them a habit. Over time, the forgetfulness will become weaker.

In the challenges of life, there is only one way to become an achiever and that is through the way. You can be found to know something about yourself when you say there is a Way. This self-knowledge is what we talked about in the fourth way. What you will find is that the victory that you find in each way is permanent. This is because they are part of the seeds of thought that the way of life is there for you. Inevitably you will be able to discover yourself in each way. In the first way of the wise, the Golden Rule, you can discover that there is a power within you that you can show the world to be compassionate. In the second way of the wise, listen with your heart, self-discovery shows us that you are not the ego in your mind, but the pulse in your heartbeat. In the third way of the wise, focus on the present, you can find that you can abide in the stillness within. In the fourth way of the wise, know yourself, you discover that you are here for the reason of self-knowledge. These ways of the wise give you the power to achieve self-discovery. This is a value of the greatest Masters. You just need to value the value of self-discovery for the work that you do to be made into an achievement. In effect, you can know more about yourself with an achievement than with money. That is what the sacred texts taught us.

Living for money is never attainable, but only can you live for your wisdom. You will become a Master of life when you practice the ways of the wise. There is no denying that practice makes perfect. There are opportunities in life to transform. There is willpower in everyone that practices. The power within you can be found in action. If you focus on achievements, not money, you receive the power necessary to transform your life. This power is about merit too. You will say, "I have received the merit." When you can do something for your life, it is greater to say, "I have this merit" rather than, "I have this money." Knowing that there is power within you is part of your transformation. Your power is limitless. When you become who you came here to be, you will find that this power will be awakened.

Sometimes the voices in our minds can tell us that we are dumb or inadequate, and you will find that this is part of the problem of human patterning, so our minds keep telling us again and again because our souls have been imprinted by these words. They damage us. We have to stop the cause of the suffering. You will discover that the main cause of your suffering is the lack of authenticity because it has been neglected and ignored by yourself and others. When you fear that you are not being authentic, you often react, rather than respond. This causes more suffering. When we resist the truth about our true nature, we suffer. There is nothing better than staying focused on achievements, not money, that can express our true nature. A key reminder of this way that the world tells you is to follow your heart.

When you focus on achievements, not money, your body, with its various parts, will be rewarded with strength and power. You will grow to love your body and respect your body when you have greater achievements. The seeds of this way of the wise that are planted can grow to become fruits in your body-consciousness. The fruits of life are produced far more by achievement than any other way. Your body is your temple for God. It keeps us constantly alive as a living organism so that we can function in perfect harmony, like music, without chaos. The musical system of the body is so perfect and powerful that by respecting our bodies we can achieve more. The acts that we repeat each day are often from the cognitive unconscious, but by bringing to light the focus on achievement, we can bring these acts of life to the light and observe our bodies with conscious awareness so that we continue to ascend into the light and climb the spiritual mountain. Your own body is an expression of God. When you express yourself from God, you can feel that achievements are well within reach. Jesus conquered death by simply allowing his body to be a temple of God. The consciousness the body attains is light. You can become pure light when you love and honor your body. You will come to love and honor God when you practice the way of achievement because all that God is, is the power within you. When you overcome the trials and the tribulations of the enemy, you will find the love within you to not deny yourself this light. You are the essence of the love you wish to be.

The five ways of the wise allow you to become a Master of life and succeed in the mastery of transformation. They are the means to get you out of Hell. What is Hell? Hell is the suffering brought on by yourself. If you follow the five simple ways, you will find happiness, and this happiness can last a lifetime. The illusion of the planet will dissolve, and the cause of

Heaven on Earth will triumph through a love of wisdom. There are noticeable impediments to wanting you to achieve, like the personal Hell that is created by human patterning and the life we are made to live with these unconscious ego patterns that define our ways of thinking, acting, and speaking. We move from Heaven to Hell, and from Hell back. We see this as a life transition. Your journey involves soul-searching. Achievement is soul-searching.

The five ways of the wise are there for you to know and respect so that you can ultimately achieve your truth. This achievement is called enlightenment in Buddhism. What is enlightenment? To recover our true self and abide in pure consciousness, with a true sense of immortality, divinity, and bliss, is enlightenment. This is called the rising above thought. Buddha says in Udana verse 49 that this is equivalent to bringing a lamp into the darkness to illuminate the material shapes of consciousness. You can always find that the enlightened person is aware of himself. It takes the true practitioner of enlightenment to be self-realized. Just focus on the achievement of each way of the wise; then you will find a truth within you that is pure and simple and a way that is governed by reason. But you must have the power of willpower, self-control, self-discipline, temperament, and attitude to follow these ways of the wise because wherever we go we will find the same unconscious patterns arise to condition us with the illusion of the world, away from our true selves until we stop following the ways of the world and follow the ways of the wise.

Do the right thing. As Buddha says in the Sutra of Hui Neng verse 2, the right action will lead you to the true Way. We learn from the prophets to overcome the ways of the world because they were not the ways of God. These five ways of the wise are the ways of God because they have been defended and demonstrated in world scripture. The illusions of the world are set up for us to stop following these ways of the wise; so willpower is the key to you living a happier and healthier life. True self living depends on these five ways. These are the ways of God that can teach you to become a Master. But life is not a battle for the warrior to fight against people and others. Life is a journey, a path that you can discover yourself and become wise. This metaphor is the truth of The Way. Dropping the unconscious metaphors of life is part of the way of the wise, and consciously creating our reality from the truths of sacred texts is how we can become a Master of life. We can stop being a warrior, but enjoy the quiet stillness of the traveler who knows happiness, which is the destination that can be achieved by following The way. The wise Masters teach us to know these ways to become the perfect embodiment of God. Only by becoming good can we embody God's goodness; then we will truly realize what the alchemist meant when he said, "You are pure, perfect, full, whole, and complete."

If you find yourself not following the ways of the wise perfectly, do not give up; repetition is the key. Since the unconscious patterns of humankind are deeply embedded in the human psyche, we need to repeat the ways of the wise many times before the ego's patterns will dissolve and we will find ourselves waking up to a life of wisdom. You can find true governance in the ways of the wise. They will give you the power to rule your life by using their wisdom to take control of the ego patterns that prompt unconscious reactions so that you can respond consciously in all situations by following the five simple ways. Life will not go the wrong way if you follow these ways. Give yourself time to know that a situation has a truth, then find the practice within your life to make that real. Do what the situation calls for.

This book will have the effect of self-development when you follow this fifth way of the wise. This is really where we are headed. These are not obstacles that you will find in your journey. You will find they are ways to overcome and grow to become a responsible, happy, authentic, and competent human being. The fourth way of the wise was the true spirit of self-development. The light came on in the quest to know yourself. This light is self-illuminating because it is the way to become conscious. When you have completely mastered the five ways of the wise, you will find your awakened "you", and the unawakened ego that unconsciously thinks, speaks, and acts will dissolve away by the light of wisdom. Learning the ways of the wise is what it means to become an awakened one. This is what Buddha's name meant, "The Awakened One". When we find our awakened self, we can say that we are wise. When you talk to your awakened self, you can find that it is alive, rather than dead.

There is a simple, but profound wisdom in the meaning of life, that you can be revealed in your wholesomeness.

The outside world usually shows us that there is a higher standard for us to achieve, as Yang-shan showed the monk what he could achieve. This shows us that we can conform to the standards of the world and rise to the occasion. When we fail to meet the world's standards, we often fail in our life completely. It is wise to listen to greater people than we are.

The thought of money always incurs a debt. Here you have found a reason for suffering. The love that we found in Yang-shan can be found in any teacher. They will have the way to set you free from this suffering because the teacher is made available for your life. The greatness of the teacher is found in the writings of Plato. When the teacher looks for opportunities for you, you can find there are paths to take. The way out of suffering is to say that you have made accomplishments in your life. Looking to the sun is bright in most people's eyes when they think they can achieve something, but we are reminded that the way out of the cave is to aspire to something greater. The light that shines within your mind propels you onwards. The way you love yourself is your power within you to achieve. When you have the mastery of self-love, you will not be longing for these cravings, desires, and attachments, but you will find wholeness and completeness in each day that you conquer. The wisdom within you will only grow within you when you achieve something great. Life is a product of your consciousness.

There is often a battle in the achievement. It propels us into a war at times with ourselves. This is so that we can see life beyond just a duration. When you start your battle, you can find the power to achieve with certain areas of focus that will bring you a greater life. We must not look to the battle as our eternal way of life, but we are shown that life itself has many ups and downs. The battle for yourself is the greatest battle that you can fight, and win, because deep within your soul is a sense of being loved and cared for by something greater. This means that you can turn your life over to that greatness. So, in the salvation of humankind, we are not alive without this sense of belonging. It is our truth that we can call being a Child of God. This makes the role of the Savior ever more powerful. Salvation is now. Do you want deliverance or indulgence from the world? Buddha remembered the wisdom and taught it for the sake of delivering the world.

When you decide to have an achievement, the life that you lead will be transformed. It is not that you don't need money to live in this world, but we know that it is not regarded by the Masters as the final love. This is the truth that seems self-evident. Money has the opportunities built right in. This is true. But there is a priority in the things that we value and in what we love. When we talk about the ways of the world being filled with money-loving people, we often say that the achievement has gone from them. They need to hold onto their efforts to achieve, more than their money. This is so that we can live in a peaceful state. We know there are efforts being made to curb the resistance of the money-loving people, and these efforts will get rewarded when we place a cooperative movement in the world.

The figures of the world are not looking very nice, so we know there is greed as a result of capitalism, and we know there is envy as well, but we haven't lost sight of the spirit that drives humankind to love, and pick up the pieces of their brokenness. This is an effort to reconcile the world unto a Savior so that the world will not be downtrodden any longer, but will find the light. He who achieves is the light unto himself. The light will only get stronger when you step aside from the ego, which is holding you back from completing the climb up the mountain in your spiritual journey. This effort to heal the world is not counterintuitive to focusing on achievements, not money. We can find again the power of intuition in this way. It is a brilliant thing, intuition. The achievements of humankind are not lost when you have the ways of wisdom. Each achievement is to the glory of the light. There is nothing that we cannot achieve if we really want to do it. Even miracles are in the wisdom. Practice the fifth way, and you will become a Master. There will be many judgements coming from yourself; then focus your attention on the achievement, not money.

The power of this transformation that you're going to experience will not stop to illuminate you soul. All the sadness and drama you experienced your whole life was rooted in not following the five ways of the wise. Hope in yourself and you will achieve more.

The Path to Freedom and Self-Mastery: Becoming A Master of Life

There is a lot of debate surrounding the topic of freedom. You can find the human need for freedom in every country. The greatest philosophers questioned whether we are indeed free. What then is freedom? Are we free or are we in chains? As Buddha said in the Sutta Nipata verse 948, "Desire is a chain that is difficult to cut off, and we are shackled to the world, but it is possible to break this chain, and once it has been cut off, there will be no more chains." The only true freedom lies in the spirit of the philosopher — it is the freedom to know you can be who you came here to be, to live authentically. The truth is that we are in chains until we know how to love ourselves. This is your chance at becoming a Master of life. Best to imitate Jesus and Socrates. It is a revelation to know how to master anything, and when you allow life to be the Master, you will find freedom.

The life that you want is here to manifest.

There is a planetary ascension in the mindset of the Path to Freedom and Self-Mastery.

This power of freedom lies in the truth of you knowing that you have a purpose. And that purpose is to heal the planet as well. This purpose is not to be decided by something outside you. It is from within. And it is within the scope of this consciousness that we call Being that we can know how to heal on a deeper, more fundamental level, so that even in the species of giraffe, koala and lion, the life force energies within them receive the soul of Creation so that they will not be set adrift. This purpose is your life's will. It is bigger than you can perceive when you are children. When you are a child, the whole world is full of opportunity, and slowly, as we get older, this opportunity turns into impossibility; so, we feel stuck or trapped as if in a cave. This is the way out, to know that you can go forward on a path to freedom and self-mastery. When you learn mastery, steer your course.

Life is the Master.

But how can you steer your course? Steering is the mechanism of the rational mind. The ancient wisdom of Plato describes how the soul is like the charioteer, with two winged horses, one good and one bad.[33] Most people's thoughts are out of control, like the bad horse, and they require proper steering to return back to balance and control. Steering is propelled by the rational mind. Reason is the heart of truth. You must not lose control of your mind, but use reason to consider the whole picture and steer to the highest level of truth possible. Distributing your emotions properly is the power of self-

---

[33] *Symposium* 246a.

consciousness. Show restraint. Living for the moment is perfect as it is. This is the heart of your journey.

That is what you are learning from the maven, how to steer your course.

The truth of life's purpose is that we have forgotten why we came here, and so forgotten how to be free. How can we recover our authenticity and be truly free? There is a power in all people. This power is the love that we find in philosophy. It turns our minds to ask questions. The philosopher's path to freedom and self-mastery is no different around the world. It is the same for all cultures. We stop ourselves from being free when we stop asking questions. Did you ever wake up and realize that you had a lot of questions to ask? Well, this is the way of freedom. The first step is to realize that everything has a purpose in life. Nothing is coincidental; there are no mistakes, and everything is part of His divine plan.

We have to ask, what then is the purpose of life? To awaken to the truth of who you are and embody the light of God so that you become enlightened by His truth. The depth of truth is alive in you so you can be free. So awakening is part of life's chief purpose. The awakening is to the glory of God. Your centeredness in Creation has the will to strive for the love of God, so this too is part of life's purpose. With this purpose, we are able to count your soul in Creation. This will birth the realization; we are here to become alive and conscious in each expression of plenitude whereby God transforms His creation into the birthright of all individuals so that they can find their heredity uncompromised by the misrepresentations that are in the play or the dream of life. This is also called overcoming the world or transcendence. In John 16:33, Jesus demonstrated this power of transcendence when he said, "I have overcome the world." The journey of transcendence is a way to the beyond. It is a matter of being convinced of the truth of immortality and imperishability. Just believe and keep pressing on upwards. Your purpose will be fulfilled with the five simple ways. The truth be told, there is certainty that you can advance with a path. Here your soul journey continues in great effort.

Here you can make your life about authenticity. Everything is possible. Looking back into our childhood, we can see that we were victims of human patterning. Plato cautioned us that the outside world patterns us with false stories as we are children. As a result of human patterning, we lose our freedom and we forget our Being. Plato wanted to protect these children from the spell of ignorance, which takes our freedom away. The spell of ignorance envelops our minds, trying to take hold of even the inner child within. Human patterning was placed within our mind's thoughts that we were not free, and we had to follow the program of life. This included following all of life's rules, codes of conduct, laws, agreements, morals and standards, but all of these ways were relative to the program and created false beliefs, whether this be the family program, the educational program, or the social program, and they were not universal, so we did not develop true beliefs which come from a universal program of truth and authenticity.

But we cannot be returned to freedom without global cooperation, which would take our subjectivity in our individual lives and bridge it over into the world so that we believe there is a world worth fighting for. The world is destined to be part of the way of cooperation, not competition, so we feel there can be a way to maneuver in this world without the fear of violence. There has never been a more profound experience than that of reconciliation. It has the truth of the way. We feel that we can protect the children's minds. This way we can recover our thoughts that we can be alive without pain. The stories that the children heard caused destruction of their souls. It was all about the soul in Plato's theory and how to heal the soul. This makes our soul better, just knowing that we can think philosophically. What was going on in our childhood was the destruction of our minds as well. When we apply the ways of wisdom to our consciousness, we can be healed mentally. The systems that caused our downfall are bigger than we are, so we have to think systemically. In the stagnation, there can only be the end of times. This means that we need to talk to each other in all branches of our lives. The powers that control these systems need to be brought into world cooperation as well. This way, we can learn to be at one with the life by making a mutual effort to participate in the world so that we can help the world heal now with helpfulness and harmony. The power to heal is in the very essence of humankind that thrives on betterment and human advancement.

We invite all people to rise up in their specific area of power to live in a cooperative environment where the systems of control talk with one another. This area of control in our own lives needs to be lessened. The world is eagerly anticipating the eyes of cooperation, which will give us the chance think philosophically and to live in a peaceful, loving, and stable environment all the time, free from the patterning of humankind. This power to think philosophically is embedded in the ways of wisdom. Awakening, therefore, has to do with philosophy, with the love of wisdom. When you turn your mind over to a philosophical thought, you can find the truth more easily. The real you comes out, when you find that you can think philosophically, because you have recovered the power of wonder. As Plato said, "Philosophy begins in wonder."[34] This is the power of the child who looks up at the stars to wonder, "Where did I come from?", "Why am I here?" and "Where am I going?" We can protect and recover the inner child with philosophy. This means the human patterning that our parents, educational systems, religious orders, and society subjected us to can be dissolved. It's time to stop the patterning of these systems and recover your freedom. It's time to be set free from the victim role that we took on as a result of being patterned as a child when we heard the lies from these false stories about our lives for the first time.

The real you, is a philosopher who loves to question the world in wonder and finds delight in investigating the sun, the moon, and the heavens in order to learn wisdom, just as the little child loves to question the world innocently and solve problems using the acquired wisdom. Perhaps the greatest question people want to

----

[34] *Theat.* 155c-d.

know is "Why are we here?" We are here to be conscious of life. The next question people wonder about is "Who are we?" We are atoms that the love has emitted within our space the thoughts that we are like human, and we believe that we are divine. One can reference the divinity from the Bible and realize that this is where we have come from too. One can say, "I am a soul," another can say "I am a spirit," and another can say "That is not correct," and they can have a discourse to shed light on this question.

Sometimes that philosopher in you comes out when you look to the sky and the stars, or the forest and the trees, or when you see a rainbow, because there is a natural tendency in all people to be like little children and wonder in the space of greatness, and feel awe, beauty, and a mystical feeling when we touch upon the questions of God. Beyond comparison, awe is something that lifts the spirit. At the heart of each of us, we are connected to the universe through a power that shows us how to know ourselves in other things. Reality was once a long time ago and now it is coming back to oneness through the will of God because it is in the understanding to have creation not in emptiness, but in the fullness of space so that all persons in humankind will know themselves as great as a mind could conceive, not outside with the bigness of Nature, but as a constituent whole, where the giving and receiving of God's love could be for your freedom. You are the fullness of space; you are everywhere, forever free. The more you search for what was lost by looking to the spiritual *logos* for it to be found, the more that reality will come back to itself through the will that desires for it to be realized. What one wonders about is the universes and gods; so that is what the mind will become.

Wonder gives us a reverence of all life.

What is life? That is the next big question to ask yourself in your steps to freedom and self-mastery. Life is identical to truth unfolding through the striving of achievement and efforts made to overcome struggle. When you begin asking these big questions, the real you comes out, and you live spontaneously in the present moment, searching for the answers, and when you find truth in your search, you feel your inner child awaken and become alive again. Philosophy, then, is the return of your innocence. This is true happiness. There is a blissful light energy of consciousness that you can feel around you when awakening; it is also called love.

What stops us from asking the big questions about life, ourselves, the universe, and God? The answer is fear. The fear that we have within us is generated by human patterning. Human patterning imprints our souls with false beliefs, so when we ask a question, we challenge the false beliefs that created our self-identity and our life story. Hope is the advancement of your life story. We fear that when we ask a question, we will lose our safety, when the truth is that our safety comes from possessing wisdom itself. We unconsciously express these patterns of identity without even realizing that many of them are false, lies, and delusions imprinted upon our souls to stop us from inquiring deeper into the nature of reality. We fail to express ourselves according to our truth. When we attempt to express ourselves by asking these big questions, we see that the people around us are not interested in the answers because they, too, have been patterned in a way that stops a philosophical inquiry into what truth is, and deeper questions like "What is purpose of life?" remain unanswered by millions of people around the world. When we start practicing philosophy, this gives us the power to talk with other people.

Because the glories of Creation still strike us with a sense of wonder, awe, and a mystical feeling of connectedness to something greater, we are sometimes reminded by a soft whisper of these questions. Open into awe. Then we begin the search for wisdom using philosophy, which is the same inner sense that made us discover the five ways of wisdom. These are the times that we feel really free and realize that without philosophy, we do not feel free. The fundamental problem is that most people live their lives without ever questioning and without having begun a dialogue of search; so, the answers that can set us free remain undiscovered. This is the same for the self. The self remains undiscovered because we fail to inquire within as to what we, as human beings, essentially are.

Love was not lost in our mind when we heard awe sound its voice. The story of our life is in the personality of the ego. So, we have to have a personal narrative to reflect our life. There are many wars that you can fight and there are many opportunities that will come to start a war. With the masteries, you can find the freedom to release yourself from the battle. The war that we choose to fight can teach us to have a personal stance, but the ways of the Masters can help you overcome what is not even personal. What you are experiencing right now is your own definition of yourself, and this is limited. So, we need to let go of the self-definitions.

The first step on the Path is to ask these questions, for this will give you the conscious awareness of there being a real truth that exists, and truth is what you are. We need to be aware that truth exists for us to be free, because without truth we do not have a chance of removing the human patterning that has us entrapped in lies. The world is full of human patterning, and if we do not ask the right questions, we will not escape the human patterning. Awareness of truth is what sets us free.

When you have the answers to life's biggest questions, you do not need to suffer. You will have lifted the veil of ignorance that kept you in chains. The love that you will find in the sense of wonder will give us an opportunity to say our truth. We will find that we can let go of these patterns easily when we know the fundamental truths of life's biggest questions, and we will no longer be made to suffer through false beliefs. Fear will also dissipate, but with truth comes security in knowing there is a greatness that can be touched. That is why it is important for you to master life. The philosopher understands this greatness, and masters life in the dialogue of search. God has placed love within you with wisdom.

To be a philosopher is a way of life. When you walk this path to freedom and self-mastery using the five ways of the wise, you are the possessor of the truths that are revealed in philosophy which constitute your way of life and have the qualities of truth and goodness within your character. This is what it means to become like God. When one chooses the five ways of the wise, one chooses to know one can become like God. The good person speaks truthfully, acts righteously, sees correctly each situation and finally, understands what is required to be a truthful person. These qualities eradicate ignorance, guiding one to happiness and spiritual progress. Each step on the Path presents the true self outwardly so that what it is inwardly can become like God. Leaving behind the mortal realm is like knowing that where you are going is higher than the mortal reality. This is the true purpose of the philosopher. Coming to know that your life is one with God is beyond acceptance. You are more than you know. To become like God is our destiny. This destiny is realized by listening to the ways of the wise that give you the power to live your truth. He or she who becomes wise recovers his or her freedom.

The path to becoming a philosopher is a path of mindfulness. What is mindfulness? Mindfulness is the state of awareness of the present, without being attached to the thoughts that arise in the moment of now and with the ability to abide in the calmness of contemplation. The practice of mindfulness is necessary because the problem of human patterning has created an entity within the mind called the ego that controls our life, shapes our identity, and controls our behavior through the unconscious patterns that were imprinted upon us as children. The ego thrives on suffering and dramas in our life story, until, through mindfulness, we are able to observe the ego as a separate entity by being the observer in our own consciousness using the "I", which is beyond observation, and detach from the entity by letting go of the ego patterns that define the false self, such as separation, rejection, isolation, fear, and loneliness. The core of the ego is the content that we have heard all our lives. This includes the rivets that are placed within the mind that identify the ego as a limited being. These patterns create our roles, such as the victim role that we live by automatically. For example, when we desire to be famous, this feeds our ego, and the role that we identified as fame will show us a clear picture of an unattainable life.

The ego is commonly thought of as an enemy within our own psyche that we must fight against, take control of, and kill. The way of overcoming the ego is not by increasing the dramatic occurrences, but by striving for peace. It is often thought that life is a battle and we must become the warrior to win against the enemy. This enemy will fall away when you choose to live from a higher mind. That is the way to conquer the enemy. There is no other way. As one attains a higher mind, one can steer and control the energies of the mind along the course of love, truth, goodness, and beauty, and away from evil inclinations of the entity, which allows the acquisition of such evils as greed, lust, anger, ignorance, and delusion. In the war of the mind, there are three powers: the power to move, the power to know, and the power to choose. We often put the power to know aside.

But life is only a battle if you let it. This is a metaphor for life. We become warriors that struggle against the entity, go into a battle using tactics, strategies, and use weapons to kill and destroy the enemy. Seeing life as a battle is part of the fundamental problem and the reason for war. The metaphor takes hold of our lives and shapes us unconsciously to act automatically as a warrior, when instead of seeing life as a battle, the greatest Masters teach that life is a journey that must be traveled along a sacred path to truth. We are travelers, not warriors. The Path is the way. This is the metaphor that we must be free from in order to realize that love, not weaponry, is the way, that peace, not war, is the way. Love is the way of the Path. We don't have to fight back because by changing our perception, we see that reality is a journey and that the way to kill the entity is by the ways of mastery on the Path.

What sort of image is the imaginary self? The monster is conceived as a many-headed beast in the ancient wisdom of Plato in his *Republic*. He says, it has "one those natures that the ancient fables tell of as that of the Chimaera or Scylla or Cerberus, and the numerous other examples that are told of many forms grown into one."[35] Plato described this shape. "Mold, then, a single shape of a manifold and many-headed beast that has a ring of heads of tame and wild beasts and can change them and cause to spring forth from itself all such growths. It is the task of the cunning artist. Join the three in one, then, so as in some sort to grow together. ... Then mold about them outside the likeness of one, that of the man, so that to anyone who is unable to look within but who can see only the external sheath it appears to be one

---

[35] Rep. 588c-e.

living creature, the man."[36] The original nature is not the beast with many heads. What is outside is different from what is within. Looking within, there are hidden parts within all people, from the truth of their mother dying, to the divorce they had, and we can find a home for each part when we confess to a higher power. Properly looking within, you must tame the lion with the virtues of courage, patience, and strength, and control the many appetites of the beast through the virtues of reason, self-control and temperance in order to stop the internal conflict and to grasp the knowledge of the true self as reason. This is so to cure the soul of evils. Philosophy is taming the beast. You will find it very difficult to tame the beast.

I wanted to remind you of the Buddhist parable in the Eastern wisdom tradition called Great Waves. It goes like this. "In the early days of the Meiji era there lived a well-known wrestler called O-nami, Great Waves. O-nami was immensely strong and knew the art of wrestling. In his private bouts he defeated even his teacher, but in public he was so bashful that his own pupils threw him. O-nami felt he should go to a Zen master for help. Hakuju, a wandering teacher, was stopping in a little temple nearby, so O-nami went to see him and told him of his trouble.

"'Great Waves is your name,'' the teacher advised,' 'so stay in this temple tonight. Imagine that you are those billows. You are no longer a wrestler who is afraid. You

---

[36] Rep. 588c-e.

are those huge waves sweeping everything before them, swallowing all in their path. Do this and you will be the greatest wrestler in the land.''

"The teacher retired. O-nami sat in meditation, trying to imagine himself as waves. He thought of many different things.

"Then gradually he turned more and more to the feelings of the waves. As the night advanced the waves became larger and larger. They swept away the flowers in their vases. Even the Buddha in the shrine was inundated. Before dawn the temple was nothing but the ebb and flow of an immense sea. In the morning the teacher found O-nami meditating, a faint smile on his face. He patted the wrestler's shoulder.

"Now nothing can disturb you," he said. 'You are the waves. You will sweep everything before you.''

"The same day O-nami entered the wrestling contests and won. After that, no one in Japan was able to defeat him."[37]

The waves will come and go, but in your heart you will remain ever-present. Did you ever wonder that your emotions were comparable to waves, and your mind was an effort to still the waves? When you feel the waves come, don't be startled.

There are three areas of mastery involved in mindfulness. First is the mastery of attention. Attention consists in the suspension of thought, so that we can notice there is a space available to be who we really are.

---

[37] Zen Flesh, Zen Bones, p. 9.

The second mastery is monitoring, which is how to observe the patterns of humankind and how to change the patterns. The third is the mastery of detachment. Detachment is what makes the transformation possible because by detaching from the ego's patterns, we can identify with our Being. The truth is that reality can only be discovered when someone is detached, so this mastery is the power of life itself that can only be revealed once one has detached from the patterns. The three actions of mastery in the transformation process allow the ego to die through the alchemy of self-love. This alchemy is essential for the symbolic death of the ego. A further solution is offered called the Initiation of the Philosopher, which is well known to the ancient schools of wisdom worldwide. But they have their fame in the Platonic and Pythagorean schools of esoteric wisdom in Greece. This initiation involves the power of practicing death so that your entity can symbolically die before you die. This is a great secret of the Masters. This is a solution that requires great courage in the pursuit of wisdom.

The masteries involved here create what all the great Mystery schools talk about when they share the paths of initiations; ego death. This is a symbolic death of everything that is not you. The opportunity to die before you die is made through your willingness to know yourself as not a figment anymore. The illusory self, dies away through the alchemy of self-love. The self is no-where to be found, yet it has an ever-present mind that says, "'I am here,'" and this mind is the Being of your truth. The truth about life and Being is able to be realized in the space of awareness that we hold within our attention a gratitude for life, love, or God. Since the philosopher is the lover of wisdom, essentially all of these masteries have to do with love. Truth is the life that you want to realize, so the plan that you have for philosophy is part of God's plan. You can win at life through the three masteries and through the alchemy of self-love. This is the skill of the philosopher. Being here now is the essence of philosophy.

Let's look at these three masteries.

The Mastery of Attention

You can learn the ways of the wise by practicing to be attentive to the life you have been given. This means that you remove your attention off the illusion, thereby placing your mind's eye into a different space of awareness. This level of awareness is increased in this movement. You will feel a higher mind set in. It is the activation of your truest potential. It is also called staying focused. We have tried to demonstrate that you need to stay focused in two ways of the wise, namely the third way of the wise, focus on the present, and the fifth way of the wise, focus on achievements, not money. The love that you find within these two ways is part of the love of the philosopher in his quest for wisdom, which is based on the power of attention. The mastery is also called the turning of the mind away from the outside world. The world is what is grasping our attention. We feel drawn to the external circumstances all day long. Part of us is dead in our lives because the power of the external world takes holds of the outside self. This means that we have to become alive again. We often need to turn our life over to a higher power. When we grasp our attention to a higher reality, we can find a higher reality called love. This is why the power of attention is so special because you can know there is love to be found.

The way the world works is that you can see only what you are made aware of. So, becoming more consciously aware of the outside world is the end of the ego. The way the mind works is that it has a love built in. By turning inward to the love within you can shut off the outside world and the outside illusion that carries on the dramas of the ego. What we want to focus on is the reality that we are pure love. This means that we must detach from the outside world. The place of freedom is in the ability to master our attention. It gives us more awareness to the love that we are sharing with God. This attention can be completely absorbed in God so that you will die in your ego faster and become reborn in your Being.

Feeling lost is not the end of the road. It is as if there is an intermission where you can gather yourself up to be more than you can be so that you can know that what was the light within is still burning.

The first step in the mastery of attention is to become aware of the language you are using and whether or not it patterns your life unconsciously with limited beliefs, or whether it reveals the true self. If you become aware of the language you are using to create your reality, you will speak more consciously with words that only affirm the truth of God's love for you. There is a reality in each word that you use, and each word can either reflect the truth or project a lie. By placing your attention on how you speak, you will learn to control your speaking patterns so that each word reflects truth and you will learn to say only what you mean to say and be honest with yourself. If you are using myths to illustrate your reality, then consciously switch from these patterns and use only words that create beauty, love, and truth. Be conscious of the way that you listen. Then the world will become alive as you define it through language. Find the love that is with wisdom in each point in your journey.

The mastery of attention requires that you hold your focus by noticing in the present what is happening around you with the light of awareness so that you can know what things are making you distracted, in order that you can return to the object of your focus. The stopping power within your mind is the love of wisdom.

This ability to know what is happening in your mind is part of your knowledge of your whereabouts. You can take hold of any kind of cognition that you want in the span of attention. Listening is the most powerful form of attention. Here you find the opportunity to tune into your life. There are times when you feel "Ah, ha moments" when you find your truth. You cannot lose this focus if you have love. There are many thoughts that will arise in this span of attention, but you have a choice to make about what to be attentive to. You can place your attention of certain objects of thought quicker than others because you care about those objects. Losing your attention to other objects is about making a shift in your awareness. This shift gives you a sense of personal power. You can drain your energy if you don't recover your personal power fast enough. The power within you is available at all times so that you can become aware of greater and greater purposes.

Life gives you this power to heal yourself. You can transform very quickly when you make a sudden shift in your attention. The power of mastery of attention gives you the right to die before you die. Your ego will die when you say "I am that" and consider yourself pure, unconditional love. So, you won't lose your Being. You will awaken. There is a key to attention. This is called monitoring. This is the second mastery of life.

The Mastery of Monitoring

In the mastery of monitoring, we take hold of each object of thought, including our beliefs, thoughts, emotions, and our judgements with our mind and observe our own thoughts and actions in the moment. It is thinking about thinking. Through the mastery of monitoring, we can know how to separate the data — what is really happening, from our interpretation of what is happening — and find the places that there are stories that are hurting our power to be who we really are. We can observe our experiences just as we experience each event and hold in our power of observation the thoughts that we are thinking, just as the thinking is taking place. This is also called watching. It is the power to hold a deep and steady intent in our thinking about thinking that allows us to become aware of the information or data. Be the watcher of your thoughts.

This is the process of knowing who we are. Knowledge is gathered. Through the mastery of monitoring, we can observe whether each thought, belief, emotion, and judgement is based on the truth of love, or is from the ego. Here, the object of thought is seen clearly with the eye of awareness or the mind's eye. By monitoring each thought, you can take a mental account of everything that is happening in your life. You can monitor the voice in your head and determine whether the voice was authentic or inauthentic, Being or not-being. The voice that affirms a complaint, like "I am not happy", is inauthentic, but authenticity is expressed without the ego's patterns. Notice that you are not the voice doing the speaking, but you are the awareness of the voice. This awareness is the true person. Listen deeply.

This power of monitoring creates a space of awareness in which you have the power to choose which thoughts to accept as part of your self-truth and which ones to reject. You can be critical with your monitoring and use reason to discriminate to know what are the healthy and unhealthy patterns of thinking. The use of critical reflection and reason is also part of your transformation. Here the method of monitoring touches the existence of your self-consciousness. That is what reason is, self-consciousness. Love will place each thought correctly. Through monitoring of your thinking, you are rigorously separating your true self away from the entity so that your self is realized as pure, perfect, full, whole, and complete. This is called self-realization.

Through the mastery of monitoring, the fear-based beliefs can be seen clearly and dropped. The mind can be totally reprogrammed with the ways of the wise so that the imprints from the patterning of humankind are dissolved and the soul can restore its original patterns and become akin to the heavenly rotations that govern the universe. You have to monitor yourself constantly, because a lot of the thoughts are not correct. See what you are attached to, and then practice letting go, the final mastery. Be careful what you think of.

When the soul recovers its heavenly patterning, the soul will know itself as pure love and the entity known as the ego will die. The revelation that truth is yourself is what observation of thinking will reveal. This is the great truth of all the Masters. And it becomes an unstoppable quest to know this truth. When you observe yourself thinking, you can apply the process of letting go more and more carefully. Allowing the time to process the observation is part of the transformation. This is so you can see how reality is created and not created. Losing your reality is not part of what is happening. The engagement to truth is as if a spell has been lifted.

When you are monitoring your thoughts, you are watching your thinking and you are watcher of the thinker. What does this exactly mean? It means that you are conscious of there being a movement in your mind that starts up your sentence structure. In the articulation of your brain, there is a voice that says your thought content to you. So, the power of monitoring shows you that you can be knowledgeable of this content and even perceive the thought forms as they arise. Through the power of choice, you can choose to identify with these thought forms or simply abide in your own consciousness and continue to practice monitoring so that all the thought forms will be under your discretion. This means that the life that you think is yours comes from a new power. "Be healthy" is the greatest thought that you can hold. Your key of life is in your monitoring.

When we have found a foundation of awareness, you will learn to witness yourself. Witness yourself making ways for yourself to live. You are the witness. There will be many areas of your life that you will make up ways, including religious ways, family ways, social ways, and so forth, but the most important ways are the ways of wisdom. But when we witness our mind, we can use discretion regarding which ways are right and wrong to follow for a better life. The five ways of the wise are the right ways because they contain the wisdom of the great spiritual Masters. Witness yourself. By crossing the darkness of ignorance, one can attain higher bliss; so, keep on, constantly awake and witness your mind.

In the space of awareness, you will find there is a place of silence that exists between the thoughts and with mastery, you can expand this space and live in this space so that you can control your thoughts, rather than being controlled by them. This is the power of meditation. As Buddha says in the Dhammapada verse 282, from meditation arises wisdom and without meditation, wisdom wanes. This is like being out of your body. You will only think when you want to think when you live in this inner space and observe the thoughts. In this space, you can feel your Being. This is also the space of creation. You are the Creator of your thoughts. Forgiveness is part of the thought process of the Creator. It is the most important thing. The soul realizes it's simple, but profound wisdom is letting go.

Since there are many rules, ethical codes, standards of behavior, and norms that we are subject to in human patterning, the next step in the mastery of monitoring is taking an inventory of what ways you are and are not, and deciding which ways to follow when you hold a new standard of truth and which ways to leave behind because they create the illusion and the worship of a false god. There could be hundreds of ways that you live by that dominate the old mindset of the ego that you might want to change so that you can live by the five simple ways. The strategies for learning are endless. So, take the easy path. It is well worth it. By letting these old ways go, we can find the truth in the grace of Love. This is called the *takeaway*. Start with the ways that cause suffering. What are they? Create your inventory and start your takeaway. With each way you take away, replace it with one of the five ways of wisdom. Looking back on your life, there are obvious cases of ego patterning that imprinted you with ways of being in the world. Try to find these patterns within yourself. This is called *looking back*. This is so you unlearn the old pattern and learn the new program. What if you could start over? What ways would help you be your best self? Falling behind is a sadness that often compels misery, but with the takeaway working effectively you will be set free.

The key to observation is detachment. The way the world works is that your self-consciousness is a reflection of the life that you are monitoring, so when you say that you want to be healthy, you have to see what is stopping you. This way, you have observed the impediment to your freedom. Careful monitoring will show you deeper truths. Your life doesn't go beyond what you look at. Learn to truly witness yourself and find authenticity.

Part of the power of monitoring lies in the ability to observe and explore alternative beliefs, such as the five ways of the wise.

The Mastery of Detachment

The mastery of detachment is the most powerful method in your transformation because it gives you the power to shift your identification away from the illusion to the truth, away from the false self, to the true self. Detachment is the gift of letting go. In this gift, we stop our mental clinging, dissolve our desires, which are often described as demons, and end our attachments to the patterns that unconsciously defined the entity for our whole lives. The decision to adopt the five ways of the wise is a decision to walk the Path of the Masters and end the identification with the imaginary self that Plato wrote about in the *Republic*. It's your choice to explore the five ways of the wise in your transformation, to help you think philosophically, and recover the truth of who you are. The stronger you become, the more you are able to discern which ways to follow in the world, and which ways to detach from. Detachment breaks the hold of the entity on our lives. When you detach, you can find the power of love more easily. It awakens you instantly to know that you have let go.

Love can give you a lot of things, but it is only the path to wisdom that can be received from the philosophy. This means that you have to detach from everything that is stopping you from being a philosopher. The choice is yours to choose to explore the possibilities of being a philosopher. There is a light of wisdom that shines eternally in the mind of the philosopher. The five ways of wisdom are there for you now to master. Practicing the five ways of the wise will make you stronger so that you can continue to walk the Path of the Masters. When you learn the five ways of the wise, you can see the demons of desire clearly and observe the cause for their existence, thereby giving you the personal power to identify with the five ways of the wise, instead of your craving. As you continue to see all the rules, codes of conduct, ethical standards, and norms we are faced with our whole life, detachment gives us the power to let go the ones that were associated with idolatry, and adopt the five ways of the wise as a way of life. If you are careful in your longings, not grasping in your desires, with a compassionate heart and pure mind, thoughtful, attentive, quiet, and composed with a single-pointed focus, with senses restrained, you will see the essential teaching of the five ways of the wise, and the essential teaching will see you. When the essential teaching reaches your knowing, you reach an imperishable, indestructible, and unconquerable state. You will not be shaken. Your mind will become illumined, bright, and pure. Becoming wise, you will be rid of all desire and be calm, unstirred by the waves.

The philosopher knows how to separate himself from the lower nature, from the anger that can boil up, and can look at himself and can gather himself up, and turn away from anger and violence. This is what is called being the watcher of your mind. This is what is required of the ruler; self-observation. When you have the correct knowledge of yourself, you can act from your true self, from the virtue in your character, not from the false self. Such a grasp of your true self requires philosophy itself.

Then you know that the philosophic nature can rule the self with moderation, courage, and wisdom. There is a deeper significance to you becoming the watcher of your mind. Your true self becomes stronger as you learn to identify with the mental formations of truth, and detach from the patterns of the ego.

By way of these three masteries, you can attain liberation. Liberation has been posited by all the major world religions. It is through the five ways of the wise that you are able to understand why you are here. Coming into your life is about remembering this truth. There are many times when we fail to see ourselves clearly. We often think we are better than people, so instead of seeing our likeness, we judge and criticize them. This puts more mental poison in our own mind, so that what we are doing to them, we are doing to ourselves. The pain we feel when we reject someone is also the pain of self-rejection. Holding onto this pain is what is causing you to not live a happy life. We have to learn to detach in all areas of life so that we can truly be set free.

There is an element of great power in detachment. When we find ourselves being selfish, greedy, arrogant, lustful, deceitful, and angry, we can use the masteries of mindfulness to help us detach from these unhealthy patterns. By constantly placing our attention on the five ways of the wise, we can observe our transformation and detach from anything that does not reflect the truth like the five ways of the wise. Love is the pattern of the ways of the wise. Through the masteries of the philosopher, you can practice detaching from any rule, code, agreement, and way that is not based on love. God has shown the ways of the wise to the prophets, so when we identify with them, we identify with their life. This means that we can transform ourselves even faster. When there is love involved in the power of prophecy, it can be involved in our lives. The more you can see the ways that are self-limiting, the more you will be able to see that the five ways of the wise represent the core truths of reality, life, the self, God, and the universe. For example, if you follow a rule that teaches you to value money over achievement, and this rule makes you greedy, the three masteries teach you how to detach from that rule and that emotion by giving you a new way of life to adopt.

You cannot end the patterning of humankind in one day. Ending our attachments to worldly things is very difficult because we have so deeply identified these worldly patterns as sustaining our inner sense, but this is part of the identification error. We have identified with the entity for so long that we need to be shown the five ways of the wise to observe that a transformation is possible. The identification error has come because we have repeated the patterning of humankind over and over again. We need to break the patterns with the power of the three masteries of mindfulness. There are many things you can detach from in your life. These include television, unhealthy music, cravings and desires that only feed the entity. You can replace these habits with good habits that will lead to happiness, such as contemplation. Through the greatness of contemplation, the mind is also rendered great. Look forward to Heaven on Earth.

Every step actualizes and heals the wounds of the true self. Your wounds call into consideration a profound mastery that can be found only in the five ways of the wise because they transport your knowledge of the world into a love of God. The inheritance of the wounds is perplexing because we have found so much freedom in the West. These wounds give us an eye for evil; so the more we heal these wounds, the more the evil will dissolve and we will come upon an era free from dysfunction.

As you practice the mastery of detachment, you will learn to pick up the self and put it down as you need it.

In love, there is nothing the mind can attach to, no matter how hard you will try; it is not possible to cling to anything in love, for the whole heart desires to unite with the other and make the other whole and complete. Love is without clinging. Love puts these clinging thoughts to rest. Desire will show you how to detach because when you are looking for your real self, you will desire only the truth.

Practice letting go so that you can realize your Being. For example, you will have to say, I forgive someone to let go of the anger, resentment, and hatred that you may feel towards a person. Be honest with yourself. Tell the truth. The consequence of truth is freedom. This is also about coming into acceptance of this person. This new thinking requires that during the question and answer process, while in the search for truth, you let go of your former self and relinquish your old identity. This means dropping the ego patterns of thought, such as selfishness, stubbornness, anger, resentment, jealousy, and hatred that defined the old identity. As things change, unfold, develop, evolve, grow, and die, the one true reality of who you really are remains unchanged, unaffected, undisturbed, and uninvolved. This is your eternal self. Soul is what the eternal reality represents. It remains free from tarnishing, defiling, and free from decay and evil. The unfolding of nature is alive with the principle of change, becoming new, becoming old, blossoming, shining, decaying, and death. Yet there is rebirth. Becoming something new is the beauty of life. Be yourself fully in the present moment, always, without sticking to the old self. Take off the old self. Put on a new self. The new self is the true self. The heroism within the doctrine of Christ is in the advent of a new you.

The philosopher attains the virtue of self-control and knows how to control himself through the masteries of mindfulness so the emotions, such as anger, do not take over the mind. The philosopher knows how to love himself deeply. This is from the alchemy of self-love. Through self-love, you can transform even deeper. This brings up many issues for many people. It takes a great conquerable mind to overcome. Love will be made available to he or she who conquers the emotions. This is the philosopher's advice to all noble disciples that walk the ways of wisdom. There are many causes of wisdom, but the ways of the wise show you that there is a world wisdom. It is wise that you find yourself in the concentration on truth, in the solitude of your study, in the peace of your mind, and in the devotion of your time to meditation so you can attain a true realization. Losing something is not possible, since it is there all along, in the light.

Remain neutral to all arisings in the body. This will increase your sense of detachment. When the pleasure comes, see that it is not to be involved with it. And when the pain comes, it can weaken your house. The power of neutrality is also in the Buddhist mind. The body is experiencing within you. It can tell you at one point, "I am free" and at another time, it can tell you that "I need assistance", and it is often the case that we find ourselves being the experience itself, so we take the body to be our selves. But this is not the truth of the term life. There is an inner self that we can discover when we are detached. Judgmental spirit will not arise. Remaining neutral is the way to stop the mind from clinging and from wandering in a disorderly motion. The mind must not wander from purpose to purpose, or be distracted from its goal and direction. When someone is doing something to affect your well-being, remaining neutral will give you the power to remain indifferent to the effects this negativity is having on your mind and body, and your neutrality will allow you to detach from the negativity. As a result, you will find your heart pure, and your Being untainted. This allows love to manifest fully.

The Alchemy of Self-Love

We turn now to alchemy to attain freedom and self-mastery. Let's look briefly at what this involves. Here the alchemy of transformation is the power of self-love. The power that knowledge has given you has, from the very beginning, made the wisdom of your soul ever more special. When you go deep into the knowledge that you have been given, there is power for self-development that begins with the magic of alchemy, which makes the attainment of freedom and self-mastery possible. You must surrender your ego to complete your journey. The self-consciousness is not going to be made right without wisdom. The ignorance that beset your mind with sorrow, confusion, sadness, and chaos will dissolve when you complete the process. This is about your transformation. Here the magic of alchemy is shown to you to heal the crisis of identity.

What is self-love? Self-love is the capacity to identify, revere, and celebrate the deepest truth of who you are. The power that you thought you had lost is in the affirmation of you being pure, perfect, full, whole, and complete. It is also not beyond knowing that you are also pure, unconditional love. The fullness of your Being is found therein. This is the truth of your authentic self. You need to stand in your own power to affirm this truth wholeheartedly. You can discover your soul with the affirmation, without which we would be dying inside. The flowering of your consciousness is in the affirmation. Do not shy away from affirming this truth on a repetitive basis. This is the essence of self-cultivation. It is here in this work that your truth will be known. The self that you saw in your mind is not complete because of the pain and suffering that you feel. So, this is why we are doing the alchemy of self-love. Your conception of yourself was flawed, but the truth is that you are here to affirm your power in knowing that you are innately good, worthy, and beautiful. The power of innateness is a revelation is the mind of the alchemist, so you cannot see it unless you know the way.

Loving yourself is the prize.

The way of knowing that you have come into Being is the truth of you knowing that you can be authentic. In your authenticity, you can claim your power back. When you make the correction to your self-concept, you will attain freedom.

The alchemy of self-love is about transforming the old into the new. You will have a rebirth. It will be like a Phoenix rising from the ashes.

Can you ever recover from the pain that you felt in your sadness? The belief in your healing is possible because the alchemy of self-love has a built-in path so you can journey to your deep self. Do not be dismayed. The efforts that you make are propelling your eyes towards your infinite Being. Virtue is the calling.

It is as if we had a human condition to begin with.

What you perceive within yourself is a multiplicity of ego patterns of thought, such as rejection, abandonment, isolation, loneliness, hatred, fear, and dread. When you see yourself as false, the goal of self-development is to say, "I am not that" so that you can turn your mind's eye away from this abuse and suffering, and shift within to a new space of awareness. This new space is not the ego. It is who you truly came here to be. It is the point of identifying yourself as not this that you can make the turn away from the outside self. This would bring your Being to the space of knowing that it is beyond repair. It is identical to the way the teacher sees you. Here the truth of yourself is not lost. The wisdom you behold in your mind is a product of self-knowledge. You want to be very careful about what you know about yourself, and state only the facts about your soul. This is so that the mind does not produce the identification error. Be mindful.

Love is not a quality or aspect of the person; it is the very meaning itself. It comes to be through a devotion to the way of truth, and not from suffering. To say you don't suffer enough is not conscious, but to say I don't love enough — that is conscious, considering that love is the very meaning of the search. But it's not just a journey to the heart that will heal you. You must say, I am present. Love comes from a change or inner transformation. The old self will be left behind. It will be brand new what you are. Let the heart's desire be the mind's desire. It is not a great loss to give up the desires of the body, as they are not highly prized, but it is a great loss to give up desires of the mind, as they are highly prized.

When you know yourself to be the love of God, this is the truest sense of an inward knowing. Then your mind will not make the identification error a second time when you find your life. Your way of self-love is the opportunity to know yourself. The feeling of your truth is essential. It is the moment that you can feel the embodiment of your wholeness. This is taken to mean that you can be aware of a state of existence. Here the feeling is fundamental in your Being. It is who you are. When we feel something, like when we adore something, it gives us an elevated sense of space so that we can move in this elevation and find happiness. To feel is to know. When we feel the light shining within our own body, we must participate in that elevation in order to shift our mind away from what is false. Here the light that is shining has become a fire that is being kindled with knowing you are magnificent.

Darkness is ignorance. Wisdom is light.

To feel is to become engaged with the sense of Being. With each power that lights the fire, we die in the ashes. This is called purification. Your mind and body will be purified by the fire of self-love. In the Garland Sutra 10, Buddha says that he has a fire that could burn up all fabrication. It is when the outside world refuses to know itself that it burns away. What is burning away? The causes of suffering, and the self is left to shine. This is called the resurrection. What you have done is remember the crucified body of the Savior Jesus. When you pour out your heart to someone like Him, you will find the means to be in a constant state of elevation. Here you become something more wonderful than you have ever been your whole life. This is what it means to revere yourself so that the brilliance of who you are can shine and be recovered.

Looking back on your history of Creation, it is true that you have never been alone. Neither has your purpose ever been gone from you. Your self-worth will be recovered with this idea. This soul-recovery is about aligning the heart right. There is a path to the heart that is revealed in the masteries. It is a straight path. When all movement is towards the essence of the soul or the Being of your nature, you will find your true self and be set free. You will be happy for no reason. There are ravines that impede the movement of the soul, which come from attachment and mental clinging, but with careful reflection and thoughtful devotion, you will find the straight path that moves you without effort, and all obstacles on your path will be overcome. The straight path is an ideal way of Being.

Compare yourself to the ideal self and know that your truth is not far away. It carries you to search for the unknown, the mystery, the transcendent, away from the curves and spirals that define the everyday world of mental chatter. It is the way of the disciplined student, who walks the Path with a silent, humble simplicity, with service to truth, and with mental order and clarity of Being. The alchemy of self-love means not straying from your sexual morality. Everything will be clear to you in the right time. Trust you are on the right path. The wise person believes the pleasures of the mind, such as the love of wisdom, are the greatest movements towards the true self, while the fool believes that the pleasures of the body are what moves the soul, and finding only obstacles in the way of the goal of perfection and becoming like God, the fool will fall to the lower levels of reality, fail in reaching perfection and not attain the godlike characteristics of divinity, immortality, and bliss, while the wise person will rise to the higher levels of reality and succeed in reaching perfection and attain the godlike characteristics of divinity, immortality, and bliss.

Find and stay on the straight path to reveal the soul's eternality and the purpose of life. It is the way of God. It is the greatest of gifts. He who knows the Path will find that it is not curved but made on truth.

It is true that the Middle Way is a foundation of alchemy. It removes the lesser world.

It is true that you are an expression of the divine. This means you are innately worthy. Self-love requires that you accept this deep truth, that you are an extension of the divine. When your transformation starts from this place, you will realize that there is nothing wrong with you. This is called waking up to the truth of who you really are. It is also called self-realization when you recognize that you are innately talented, strong, worthy, whole, and unique. Self-love is the healing power within you. There is a transformation that will take place with self-love.

When you think of loving yourself, we must return to the path of the heart.

The heart-space is often illustrated as a castle, temple, or cathedral. There are sacred places of the world that are mirrored within your own body. There are doors through which you can enter, including a doorway of the heart. Deep within your calling is the power to go through the doorway of the cathedral. You have the power to choose to enter. A doorway is often believed to be the way to God. A doorway allows you to enter into the sacred heart-space to search for the wisdom of the heart and heal the pain of your heart. By transcending the mind, you enter into the timeless, space-less, pure present where pure unconditional love flows to the soul from God. Search the heart-space. Check to see if something is written there within your heart. When you experience a heart opening, you can discover the transcendent truth of the Supreme Self, known as Atman, Buddha or Christ, within the heart center, which is the Lord of the true self. You can transmute the energies of the past to become pure light with the fires of self-love. This can be discovered by seeking to know how to love oneself. The heart-space is not an illusion, but a truth of the human psyche that holds that internal spaces within oneself can be explored and discovered, and with patience, the depth of the heart can be known. The path of the heart is infinite.

How many days are there that you do not remember you true self? Those are the number of days that God says, He is there. What do you want to remember? The sunlight upon the ocean? The stars in the midnight sky? The flowers blooming in the field? Or the light that shines in and through all these things? What can anyone give you that is better than this light? Starting here, right now, that light is shining as you turn around to perceive the truth of God's presence. Be one with this light. The person who lives in the light of God remains present with eternity. Only this moment is real and it is the door to the divine. Listen inward deeply and sense the true power of Being. Here, the heart speaks. When you know you can concentrate on the heart-space, the entrance into the cathedral is easy and nothing will dominate you. This gives you a chance to communicate your heart's desires when you walk through.

When you choose to align yourself with your Being, you will affirm, "I care about myself deeply."

The wise disciple will enter the secret chamber of his heart and start the journey along the sacred Path, conquering all obstacles, mastering all fates, and accomplishing all goals to achieve the kind of perfection that was before only known to the gods. We know the power of the disciple in many initiation traditions; he dissolved the darkness of self-ignorance, and finding the true self to be there, in the center of the heart, he felt a spiritual transformation and attained enlightenment with the path of the heart. Freedom will come to those that are full of heart.

The more we practice the three masteries, the more we can be conscious of ourselves. Our personal consciousness is governed by our self-awareness. The more we can be aware of the truth of our own magnificence, the more we will be aware of the divine spark that was placed within our Being. As you practice shifting your focus within your span of attention to this place of pure Being, the more the energy shifts and the ego patterns of thought dissolve. Anything that is a distortion of our original nature cannot exist within the space of self-love. This is the alchemy part. All our cells within our personal consciousness will transform according to our personal belief system. If we believe we are magnificent, we will become aware of this truth within our lives. When we become aware of our essence, our bodies and biology will respond accordingly. The more we become aware of our innate worthiness and our innate goodness, our personal vibration will change as we draw in higher energies of self-love, and through the law of attraction, the old ego patterns will die away and the new patterns of perfection, goodness, and beauty will materialize. The day that you would realize you're beautiful, it is because you have found forgiveness.

There are many values we have in the world, including spiritual, family, national, educational, and social values, but the most important are the ones we have for ourselves. These are called our inner values, and it is these that we must pay attention to. We must look inside. These include authenticity, sobriety, physical exercise, work, talent, strength, self-esteem, mental health, independence, energy, attractiveness, belonging, and accomplishment. The interactions we have with ourselves depend on these inner values. Values can help you make the creative improvements needed for self-development. The love that you need will come from these values.

The truth is that the illusion of the outside world cultivates a distortion in our thinking. This original distortion makes us feel that we are not worthy or good, but through spiritual evolution, we awaken to realize that we are not separate from God, but we are one with Him. You're going to feel the light within. The illusion of separation dies when you surrender your ego. The happier we will be through kindness to ourselves, and the more beautiful we will feel. The essence of self-love is to be aware. When we attend to our self, and get to the heart-beat of self-love, we can be healed. This is called living in spirit.

There is a light that shines in everybody.

The Initiation Of The Philosopher
A final solution proposed in self-transformation is the Initiation of the Philosopher. This allows you to experience a symbolic death of the entity known as the

ego. In ancient wisdom, Plato said in *Phaedo* that the practice of philosophy is the practice of dying before you die.[38] Death is our teacher.

But what is death? Death is a creative force that separates the true self from the entity that has ruled our whole life according to egoistic patterns. The true disciple must empty the self totally of these egoistic patterns and practice to die before you die. This is called self-emptying. In the Tao Te Ching verse 22, it says, "To be empty is to be full." Emptying yourself is the spiritual practice of finding the true self. This is the way of poverty; it is to know yourself as nothing. This is not a limitation to your being that predicates your soul with weakness, wounds, and impoverishment. There is no means to heal the brokenness within the evil of a death-consumed culture. This brokenness is an opportunity for transcendence of the world and its projection of the self as limited in time and space. Live in faith. Face your wounds, own your poverty, and transcend each projection of weakness with self-knowledge of the true self as untouchable, indestructible, incorruptible, and unbroken. Then healing and restoration can take place.

Those who walk in poverty and emptiness will truly know the fullness and wholeness of the divine nature within and can truly surrender in love to a more heavenly perfection. Right here is paradise. It's a perfection only God could dream of. This state becomes identical to God's abiding and infinite fullness. Ultimately, the ways

---

[38] Phaedo 64a3-4.

of masteries are the ways of death. Death is unknown. This is the way to freedom, not suffering. When we are faced with death, we fear what is going to happen. The masteries teach us not to fear, but to face death with courage. It is important to be strong in the face of an imminent death, because death will be real for you at any time.

What happens when we die? There is no such thing as death. It is part of the illusion of the self-consciousness. The life is with you, and knowing the ways of mastery has put you on the Path to attaining a true realization of the bodiless existence. The knowledge that you have attained in these lessons is invaluable to your presence at hand. The wisdom is within.

We master life by letting go of death. Although endings are part of life, such as the end of a relationship, a career, or within a life transition, we must not live in the past. Letting go is very important. Angelic support is there for you.

The purification of the mind is essential to self-development. The noble disciple will practice attention, monitoring and detachment to purify the mind. When you master the senses and become liberated from sensory lusts, you will ascend into the intelligible world where intellectual pleasures give rise to wisdom and higher wisdom with the love of learning. When the senses master you, you will be led astray. The ego will die when you practice these masteries, and there will be rebirth of the true self in a spiritual body. This is a process of stilling the mind. The mind must be stopped. So, it is no different from dying. The emptiness is stillness, an ego death. There is no more person. It is absolute self-negation, self-annihilation, and it is the presence of the Absolute itself.

Dying before you die is necessary because the false self stands against God.

This absence of the self is the experience of transcendence. The noble disciple will strive to become pure of heart and mind through the conscious act of letting go of all things bodily in order to return to his or her true self, which is pure already. It is not easy to practice philosophy when you learn the five ways of the wise, because the old egoistic patterns will try to stop you attaining this knowledge. The ego does not want to die. And we feel that death is going to take our life. When we live with the ego's patterns, it is as if we are already dead.

This practice is about inner freedom and transcending all possibilities and limitations of the ego in order to dissolve the false self. Truth is undying. It takes mastery to face this symbolic death and overcome. Realizing the true self is eternal, immortal, and divine. This practice prepares the soul for service to help the less fortunate and to serve God. The emphasis is placed on the disciple's becoming like God, who is naturally pure, so the disciple must die to the false self and release every attachment within the false self, therefore experiencing death. The self that is destroyed is the created self that is reborn. This makes everything alive again. This is the process of becoming like God and everlasting life. In the emptiness of mind, you can find your divine nature. The God-mind will manifest in the renewing of your mind. The old mind must die. It must be still, and it must cease, in order for the renewal to take place and for you to attain freedom and self-mastery.

It is true that you are of the nature to die to the false self, and be reborn. But Being will never die. It is the resurrected self. Christ was the resurrection. The egoistic patterns will die forever, along with the ego. This is what philosophy does for your transformation. It is the lack of self-control that makes you feel that you are not with eternality, and when you have self-control, you have eternality. This is called temperance. It is the essence of philosophic virtue. Your death that you find unconquerable is really conquered in philosophy so that you can realize that you are with the eternal seed of life. You can find your seed of life in the philosophy of the five ways of life because it gives you a connection to truth through the sacred wisdom. The light is here for you to realize. We are here to find our light. Each of us is a ray of light. Death is not something that you should fear, because you are the eternal light itself. This means that you have within you God. There is an indwelling power within the divine center of the deep self. In a most mysterious manner, you are able to directly know the reality and truth of purity, perfection, wholeness, completeness, and fullness. The truth of these perfect ideals is what makes the real self, akin to God. The eternal place of self-love is like God knowing Himself. Hold onto the love for who you are.

When you pass this initiation, you will meet the true self.

The New Era of Wisdom
Heaven on Earth

I want you to create for yourself a new life story that begins with the truth of God's creation. This is a new vision for yourself, a new life, and a new understanding. The vision you had of yourself your whole life was not part of God's reality. Why not create for yourself a new vision that is not like the one you had of yourself your whole life, but is different? Try to do this wholeheartedly. The truth of the Second Coming of the Messiah is that there will be a radiant blaze that shatters all the ways that were forlorn. You have the power to change this old vision of yourself by consciously creating for yourself a new story of "me". You have the power to envision your belongingness to Heaven and your belongingness to God so that you can reconnect yourself to God. This is the beginning of your path to God. In the new era of wisdom, we can find Heaven on Earth. Christ was called Wisdom.

You are in the Great Chain of Being. This is nothing that you cannot enjoy in this vision. As Buddha said, "A snowflake never falls in the wrong place."

Start by closing your eyes and imagining the truth that you are a Child of God by using your mind, your imagination, and your emotions to create a vision of Heaven. Coming to affirm this reality is about coming out of the darkness. Do what the Creator asks of you. Speak precisely and listen deeply. Listening can broaden your awareness. So that what you're thinking can be transformed through the alchemy of self-love. Imagining the true nature of your soul requires that you actually make an image of your soul, and when the image of your soul is perfect, your soul will resemble the perfection of God.

What do you see? The path of imagining is the path of concentration. Concentrate on what you see; look into yourself with greater concentration. This is the work of a clever artist, who can create a false image or a true likeness of the soul. Do you see the human image of yourself, or do you see a divine image? What image is created? Capture the reality of your soul as if in a painting. Put all else out of your mind. Give the image of what you actually see proper consideration, forgetting everything else that has been seen before your eyes. Every person is an artist and dreams up their truth through art. Is your soul a wild soul, with deserts, forests, oceans, rivers, grasslands, and mountains? Maybe it is an image of a butterfly, a flower, a star, or a sea, that takes you to your truth. Whatever it may be, by letting the imagination take hold, you can consciously undo the shapes that were put into your soul that distorted the self, rather than leaving it an image of beauty, truth, and goodness, instead creating an image of falsehood, and evil. Soul-shaping is what the unconscious forces do through language, but with alertness, attention, and thoughtfulness of mind, you can transcend the power of language and return to the soul's original purity. What image does God see of you when He is looking at you? A poor person, or a rich person? Hopeless or needy? Brokenness? Lack of love? The image that God sees of you is an image of Himself. Concentrate only on this image, then you find the truth of who you were meant to be. Say aloud, "I am a Child of God." This truth will open up your spiritual eyes so that you can see clearly the truth that God placed within your heart. Stand in your own truth.

He has placed the seed of life within you so you can find it. This is the reality that God wants you to know. Now hold onto this vision as you choose to believe in the truth of creation and the truth that you are made in God's image. Say aloud, "I believe in God." Now that you have your vision and your belief, practice self-discovery to look within to know the truth of your being pure, perfect, full, whole, and complete. You can know yourself by comparing the picture of Heaven and the true self to the picture of Hell and the false self. Grasp this truth with the eye of your soul so that you have a new understanding. Do the work.

What is going to save you? The wise man says, "You must follow the ways of wisdom." It is the palate of superiority, and the profession of life is wise. The land that you ploughed in order to become anew is fruitful in the eye of transformation; so, it is this way that the wise people need to grasp. It is in becoming anew that you sacrifice the ignorant self for the path of the wise. This makes you responsible for Being.

This is the evolution of consciousness. We know there are many stages in humankind. The stage of life. The stage of infancy. The stage of childhood. The stage of being an adult. The stage of the elderly. The stage of death. The stage of going beyond death. In each stage, there is a revelation that contains the seed of each face so that you can know there is a way of overcoming. We see the face called the Effervescent or the Shining as a pure conscious state. This even may be called pure consciousness. It invokes the evolution therein. So, evolve.

This reality is based on Heaven so you will ascend to a higher place in your heart. But it is not just here that you want this truth to be known. It is in all places. You can see the world with the same beauty that you have dreamed for yourself. God wills for you to live this life so that you can be his child and that the doors may open forever into His Kingdom, so that you may be led deeper into the Mysteries of His face, without which you can only call that way that you were going "lost", and that part of yourself "dead".

This is the path of life that will lead you home. It's in you to conceive of your truth. Do not worry. It's far more beautiful than you have ever imagined. To be beautiful, a thing must be perfect, and to be perfect it must be all-inclusive of things that belong to its own kind. Surely you see that God's face was the most beautiful. And by gazing upon His face, you can see love in all faces, just as the alchemist could see. You will be overflowing with love.

This picture that you created for yourself is not just a story. It has the element of being a reality because you believe. This is the most important step to attaining Heaven on Earth.

You can touch the love of the universe and see that all of creation is rendered more pure, with your vision of Heaven. Here in the spiritual dimension is eternity. It's in a vision that you can see, not in a place or time, and God would allow you to perceive so that you could attain knowledge by way of the faculty of sight, which is far superior to other faculties, and God put reason into sight so that you could understand truth. This faculty is not to be underestimated because with it, you can see the light. And light will be attained in this faculty of knowing. This is called enlightenment.

There is a planet Earth to consider. Waking up is building upon the way, the truth, and the life that you found to be realizable and tellable to the world.

Having a vision of reality is like a light that shines in the dark. It is an eternal light called Being. It is not negated by what is false, but is eternally present. It has within it the light to help you see the truth. Coming into this light is your enlightenment. You can perceive "'what is'" with the light of "'what is".' Then you will apprehend the Good and know the reality behind the masks. It has your soul-truth within it. Before enlightenment, the soul exists in the world of images. The mind is filled with distractions, confusion, clutter, and chaos. Boredom is confusion in the mind. The boredom that people feel can be lifted with the great wisdom. The thought forms in the mind can be transcended. This is freedom. And this light is comparable to the heavenly realms where God has planted the truth of his reality. And the life on planet earth will be healed by this light.

In the plenitude of the era of wisdom, we can count on knowing that there is a reality worth fighting for.

There is a key to the spiritual dimension. Let me remind you that for the Buddhist, this way of creating Heaven on Earth was comparable to the great journey we are on. Let me remind you of the Buddhist parable called Open Your Own Treasure House.

"Daiju visited the master Baso in China. Baso asked: "What do you seek?"

"Enlightenment," replied Daiju.

"You have your own treasure house. Why do you search outside?" Baso asked.

Daiju inquired: "Where is my treasure house?"

Baso answered: "What you are asking me is your treasure house."

Daiju was enlightened! Ever after he urged his friends: "Open your own treasure house and use those treasures."[39]

Heaven on Earth is within. You can feel the truth within you.

Your freedom will give you the power to live without constraint. Through this freedom, you can find the power of self-expression. This is the power to realize the truth of who you are in all situations, with the consent to be yourself fully, and for others to be themselves fully,

---

[39] Zen Flesh, Zen Bones, p. 25.

without justification for your self-expression, self-development, and self-confidence. Revealing why you came here is part of God's plan.

The one indwelling life essence or spirit takes the love of God higher. It is found in the life-forms of each heavenly thought. The life-forms exude a kind of truth to them, and this propels the love of the Universal Self. All the creatures in nature have the part to play in the heavenly mind. Nature was the first garden for humankind in the Creation of earth. You can imagine that there is a natural wisdom in Creation that we can recover in our effort to be still. What the birds can conceive, we too can feel. What the world is to nature now is to tame the wild, but we have to allow nature to be powerful to assume a balance. This is the essence of power.

How should we live? It is a question that encompasses every way of the wise.

Do you want to live alone and find the world gone from you, or do you want to busy yourself with kindness? On the one hand, we can say that solitude awakens the ways of wisdom, but on the other hand, the eye of kindness is the full revering of humankind.

Your life affirmation repeats the song of life.

The perception that you had of all people will be changed. Instead of seeing the illusion, you can see as the alchemist sees, that they too share in the reality of God. They are really pure, unconditional love as well. Their truth may just be hidden. The love that is coming out from you is perceivable by all people; so, they too will see and feel this love that you are radiating. Their reality can become newness as well. The eye of awareness that sees Heaven is truth. Truth is the mind. You can find a new life in this truth. Peace comes upon the soul more quickly with the thought that life was not born here to die, but was to be given a newness, and a new self. Find the pot of gold. The "me" that you were is no longer. That was God's wisdom known to the philosopher, and none could take it from Being. What was once real long ago is now coming. Turn your eyes upon philosophy. These will give you a perception of Heaven on Earth, and the start of a new life. Philosophy will separate the impure from the pure, the mortal from the immortal, the destructible from the indestructible, and the corruptible from the incorruptible.

Make a promise to yourself to live truthfully. This promise is the most powerful thing you can make with yourself. It is the beginning of the end of all lies, delusions, and falsities. It will give you the permission to live a happy life. This is why you are here, to have a promise of this making. Your power of identification is in the promise. What you choose to identify with is God in this version of your life story. This is, in effect, the power to drop the mindset of evil as you choose to go deeper into the reality of truth. Love is the power of the promise with the true self. This promise gives you total acceptance, approval, and recognition of your Being. This will free you from internal conflict, and conflict with others. By approving the truths in the essential teachings to be your truth, you consciously create for yourself a new self-understanding that outwardly will be peaceful to all people. It is your choice of peace that is the greatest achievement. You can find peace abounding in every heavenly sense in God's truth. Love and peace are here for an eternity when you choose to acknowledge the truth of who you are, and the truth of all people. This is total acceptance of their selves as well. You can continue to revitalize this vision of Heaven with your imagination. You can continue to live in this reality for an eternity because God has made it His reality.

With the five ways of the wise, you can make your dreams come true.

This agreement with yourself to live truthfully sets you free from the fear of self-expression. You will be free to affirm life by saying "yes" to everything that allows this fundamental promise to exist and "no" to everything that comes into conflict with this promise. The fear will be dissolved, and so will the mental poisons of hatred, aggression, greed, selfishness, pride, and delusion. Your heart is free from the judgement of others and self-judgement. This comes from the promise that you made with yourself, which is the total acceptance of yourself unconditionally. This means that you also love yourself. When you have found the freedom from interference to live your life truthfully, the desire to control other people will also be dissolved, for your internal freedom will give permission for other people to be themselves fully. You can be wise in all the areas of philosophy, but none is more wise than in the area of God. Your soul is going to a higher plane of existence when you focus on God. You have found the life within you to be heaven-bound. But this is not just your imagination. This is your truth.

The truth of your reality is based on self-love. Heaven on earth is to be and to live in love. When you have found this within you, you can heal the world with your confident self-expression that emanates oneness with God. Love is what you are trying to realize in your vision. You can send this love to the trees, the mountains, the animals, other people, to the sky, to the birds, and to the lakes and oceans. There is a frequency change within you when you focus on self-love. You will take charge of your life to respect other people, value other people, and to not reject them based on their beliefs, judgements, and ways of living. You will be able to say "I love you" without conditions, meaning that they do not have to do anything to deserve your love or earn your love. You will say these words without the fear of rejection and shame. This is the meaning of pure, unconditional love.

Your vision of Heaven includes the spiritual values of respect, kindness, love, peace, friendship, beauty, animal life, learning, caring, and freedom. When you imagine these values as being part of your life, you will find that the picture of Heaven becomes more beautiful. The greatest truth that you will realize is that you are immortal. This glimpse into your eternality is part of the vision of Heaven. This means that you will stop fearing death. You realized the song of immortality in the music of the spheres. It is an eternity that is contained within the seed of life. This eternity has within it a sound. The ancient wisdom of Plato reminds us that there is a chorus of philosophers that continue on the right notes of temperance, wisdom, and justice so that the true nature of the soul is to be filled with secret music.[40] Let the sound resonate within your mind so that you can be attuned to the chorus itself. It is sung in a world that is beyond this world. Let the minds of those in song be praised for their light. He who finds the tuning fork to become one with the light can also become one with God. They sing to awaken you. It's their mind that is a melody and their heart that is a rhythm. The song can be told to be the mind of love. In my world, all that remains is the triumphant call to dance, rising up like the brightest sun. Nothing is impossible. This rising up of your soul is because of grace. Each resounding sound of the music is bringing you into a state of bliss. Musical concord is brought to you through love.

For this vision to become a reality, you must believe with all your heart that it is possible. This will take you above the world of lies, falsities, and delusions, because you have started a way into faith. Faith will take you to the love of wisdom of the philosopher. When you have faith, you cannot lose the vision at all, because you believe. What the Masters of life gave to you is sacred wisdom revealed in the scriptures. This gives you the evidence needed to know how to anchor your true belief in God's reality so that you can understand the truth of who you are and of God's Creation.

It is possible to live this life of Heaven on Earth all the time, without fluctuation, by not deviating away from the wisdom of the five ways and not going away from

---

[40] Rep. 491c.

God's Path. You can start living the five ways of wisdom by putting them into practice every day of your life. The five ways of the wise make your life more and more simple because they show you the truth of who you really are. Have knowledge of every way, then show up for living that way. You can have reality mirrored in the most enlightened people, and what we have given you in the Path to Freedom and Self-Mastery, so you can be there too. They live in happiness because they follow the five ways of the wise, which gives them a different perception from what the patterning of humankind allowed them to hold. They attain self-mastery through these ways alone. With just one glimpse of the truth of God's Creation, you will know that Heaven on Earth is real. It requires effort to hold onto your Being and the reality of Heaven on Earth. Truth was there in each effort. The effort is what is the truth. Because of this great and honorable effort, you would not have to save yourselves from the ignorance that beset humankind in the beginning, but you would be saved by your belief in God.

When we think of Heaven on Earth, we think of the way Jesus conveyed it to us and how he showed it to us in his words and his works for the Creator. Jesus said in Colossians 3:2, "Set your minds on things above, not on earthly things," and we are told in Philippians 3:20, "But our citizenship is in Heaven. And we eagerly await a Savior from there, the Lord Jesus Christ." The message of eternal life is really what He was preaching. This reality is still alive. The messages of truth, goodness, beauty, and love are in your unshakeable faith. It would take that long, maybe even a lifetime, to put your true self with God, but with faith, it could be made right, and you could be shown the same vision you had when you were created. It is God's will for you that you would come to know the right way. So, you could be set free. What is life to you? Think about this question and feel alive. Live in faith. Let your faith be like a dawning of a day in which you can arise and awaken. Be yourself fully.

The truth be told, there is great beauty in the world. You can see the beautiful sights and sounds in the world, and when you perceive the face of The Beautiful, you will see that they too must participate in the Mystery of God and be reflections of His greatness. By living according to love, you will find that your soul is healed from the delusions that were put there by human patterning. You have been given a chance to decide and you have an impeccable person within you, so by making the right choice, you can live the life you decide. There are choices each day pertaining to life that you are confronted with. You have to look into your impeccability and realize that it is your goodness that is at stake. Look into your own mind. This means you can't go the wrong way or else you will be one of the fallen. It has pains and sufferings in this state. No one knows where that emptiness comes from, but surely it is part of making the wrong decision. What was once alive in you could go the wrong way. Best if you know yourself, then you will have the courage to steer the course. This has to do with knowing that the outcome has to do with your impeccability. Realizing there's no difference between you and your choice is about saying that your life is here to be what you say it is. This is why it is necessary to make the best choice possible in every situation.

It is not possible to even hate once you have attained the Christ-like mind. You will have shut off these fears within you. You will naturally be inclined to love from a Christ-like perspective. Happiness will result from this action, and love will continue to flow from a pure heart. Happiness cannot be found from outside or from the inside. It simply is, always. Once you decide to love like Christ, the reality will be pure at all times. There will be no more confusion about what is real, or who is saying what. The world will be pure bliss. This is the reality of Christ being incarnate in your life. All the world will smile at you. Your difficulties in thinking, concentration and forming thoughts will be healed. Your thinking will no longer be muddled or impaired. You will remember things better, and your thoughts will not seem like a cloud.

What you have been waiting for has revealed itself through the five ways of the wise. The sacred verses were written a long time ago; so, we have seen an evolution of humankind since then, but at the pinnacle of humanity, there remains the truth that happiness is far better with God. Our evolution has come into our self-consciousness, making us available to transformation. Although 2,000 years have gone by since Christ came, it is still possible to find his light on the planet. This means that happiness is about His transforming us.

The journey to Heaven on Earth is fully attainable.

We are left with this vision of Heaven on earth to remove the imprints of human patterning. We have within our mind the power to create something anew. This is exactly what humanity needs to create a brighter and more sustainable future. When you see the light, your light will grow on the planet when you start to practice the five ways of the wise consciously. Heaven is the conscious evolution of humankind. In the Anguttara Nikaya verse 3.22, Buddha called this state Nirvana because this is the calm from all the mind's impulses, and the extinction of dispassion and impulses. The love you find within Buddhism is not relative but has the permission for you to be the love of God. Life itself is in this evolution, so we can be made available to a transformation being made in the consciousness of humankind when we believe in this vision and follow the five ways of the wise to manifest this vision.

The cloud of confusion has been in your mind all your life because of the problem of human patterning, but it can dissipate with this transformation, along with the entity that contains all your false beliefs, false judgements and false perception about yourself, others, God, and about reality. The false self will produce a distorted image of God. If there is a false self, there is a false God. The false self divides us from God by projecting a false sense of personhood that is kept alive with an idol. With a false God, there is false judgement. You must worship a true God. You must correct your ideas about God through the power of belief. Believing what is true is the way of the heart and the way of real love. Because your false belief is holding you captive as if imprisoned in a cave, you are attached to the entity that believes in the illusion because it has imprinted these false beliefs so deeply in the human psyche. This makes letting go of the old patterning difficult. It requires conscious awareness to let go and surrender the entity called the ego so that you can identify with the true self by following the five ways of the wise. It requires you making a choice each day to believe in God, to know yourself, and to follow the wisdom of the Masters so that you can live a better life and attain self-mastery.

The attachment to the ego creates needless suffering, but we are comfortable suffering because our whole lives have been about suffering. We must choose not to suffer and choose to live in a state of bliss all the time. Life is a series of choices. When you make one choice, your perception changes, and so does your reality. When you choose to be happy, you will see yourself as beautiful, healthy, and wise, and your reality will reflect this goodness. When you choose to suffer, you will see yourself as ugly, unhealthy, and stupid, and your reality will reflect evil. There are no good reasons to suffer.

You can practice the five ways of the wise consciously all day long. This is called living the five ways in the new consciousness of Heaven on Earth. Be part of creating a new movement around the world for living the five ways. They are convenient and easy to practice. This makes finding happiness simple and very possible to attain. You can live error-free when you correct your vision about yourself. This is only possible by seeing yourself as a Child of God. The essence that you seek of yourself is reflected in how you are made; you are made in the image of God. The essence gives you the power to know the brightest region of Being. This reveals your inner divinity and the truth of your original nature, which is told by the five ways of the wise. The five ways of the wise recover your power to choose to live freely with God. They are simple and yet effective tools to come back into happiness, into joy.

You are empowered with these ways of wisdom. They take your power back and teach you how to affirm your life with truth. When you know this is your life, you can find your truth easier. When you affirm your life, you can choose heaven easily. This is the choice of the Masters, and they have given this power of choice to you by showing you the vision of love they knew was possible for everyone. You are the vision of love. You are the vision of truth. And you are the vision of hope for so many people that continue to struggle with the patterning of humankind and the illusion of the outside world. So, when you choose the five ways of the wise, see that they have led you to heal the planet. Jesus chose the vision of Heaven. Will you choose to follow Him?

"What does the future hold?" The future holds the promise that there is an awakening that you can be made aware of, to shatter the evil of there being no self to begin with, when we have identified, in the very consciousness of the minds of truth, that there is a likeness to God within the sons and daughters being considered for the new program, which calls them into mindset of the abolition of totalitarianism. So, we take hold of this future in our right thinking and mold ourselves into a greater human connectivity for there to be an awakening that will shift our minds into this abolition process. When we are conscious of a need to be greater than we thought we were, we can rise up and take hold of the vision of Heaven on Earth so that all the hearts and minds that we are connected to have planetary healing. This makes the world a better place when we consider the downfall of outside, and the truth of the great Kingdom that Jesus placed within.

We often wonder whether life is worth living when we see such a grandiose vision. We top off our life with excessive luxuries and fill our closets in an effort to sustain His grace, and life can be filled with travels, but the real effort is to take the meaning from our adventure and incarnate the love of Jesus. Then there can be a self-realization. Then the effort to live freely will be lifted and the new program of human consciousness will start.

The goal of Heaven on Earth is to heal the world. This can only come when we drop our selfishness, and look to a greater vision of life. This includes removing the "me" and the "mine". That is an invitation to adopt these five ways to change your way of life for the better and to practice. Then you will unlearn all those previous ways that created conflict in your mind. You will have peace. Just live according to the five ways.

Your sense of adventure has just begun when you feel this sense of newness.

Here the goal of love is to retain this newness so that you can feel a complete transformation. Welcoming this life will give you your potential to make this reality happen. It all comes down to your power to behold the truth. This is so that Heaven on Earth can be materialized. It is about the love that you can retain for yourself which will envelop your soul in the cosmos so that the earth can be lighter with the loss of the ego. This means that the earth will evolve with your awakening, and this is the benefit of all humankind. Here the life that you want is true, good, and beautiful.

Know you are the light of the world; therefore, you are the sun of wisdom.

Your journey is now complete.

Prayers
Prayer for Freedom

Lord, The Creator, we ask for your presence today to share in a communion of love, so that all that we can be is with You in the depth of your love divine, because we know your Almighty truth is that you are the Beloved and in you, I exist, I shine. The rivers declare your perfection, and the seas say Holy is your name, the West and the East, and the North and the South are governed by you, and the sun and the moon were placed in the sky so that we could admire your magnificence. There is none that compares to your love. It is pure, perfect, full, whole, and complete, just as you told me I am. Here I am standing in your presence with an open heart to be led into Heaven, and I share with you my soul. With my soul here, I am eager to fulfill the five ways of the wise, so that I may become alive in your presence, and no one can stop me. Here I am, and I pronounce your name "I Am". The heavens declare this my victory. Teach me to know the five ways of the wise for all time, so that my heart will continue to overflow with love. For I know that I am the truth that you called me to be, a Child of God. Your love will not go from me today because I promise that I will be a constant reflection of your truth, and this truth is without conditions. Show me the works of your love are here for me so that I can create Heaven on Earth with you. Show me the wickedness of the Enemy is no longer affecting my soul, and with your clarity I can realize how deep my love goes. Here I am in your presence offering my life to you so that I may become the Life. Loving all others is something I know how to do because of you. This is where you have brought me today into the love of your Beauty so that I will find rest in knowing that you paid the price for my life. Teach me that these five ways of the wise are for the land of the righteous. Perfect are you in all your ways. Love will never be taken from me when I understand your nature. It is for this that I have come here today to seek an understanding. Will you replenish my emptiness that I thought was me? Will you bring me the fullness that I believe to be me now? This is the emptiness that I gave away today. It contained all the myriad of evils. Thank you for washing me clean. This is the fullness that I have received. I will not reject you ever again, but give up stubbornness, animosity, selfishness, greed, anger, resentment, blame, self-punishment, pride, and hatred. Your love is without conditions, which you have taught me that I am. Here I am standing in your presence to reveal the truth of my new self and the start of my new life so that we can be together as one. This is why I have come here today to say, "I love you." The meaning of these words is deeper now because there is truth in me. I have felt your presence with me in my love for wisdom, so I honor your work in my life today. Your love brought me this life; so, I choose to live for you. I allow myself to be used by you in my body, in my mind, in my soul, and in my spirit. Here is the person that I have become. Show me how to become like you by using the five ways of the wise, for surely, they are in the depth of your heart. I allow you to rule my heart as I continue on my way to love you with the fullness of wisdom. Thank you for the truth that you have placed within me and for the freedom to be alive as you made me. AMEN

Prayer for Love

We are going to become alive in this world so that all our thoughts become reality right before our eyes. We will paint a beautiful picture of this world with our imagination so that we can create this beauty together with love all the time. In this picture, you traveled back in time to the Garden of Eden, to a time when you could hear the sound of birds, the flowing river and the voice of God speak to you. You walk to God and stand in his presence and you see that from His presence comes a light that fills the whole of creation with the most beautiful colors of life. You see the immensity of light pouring like water into the forests and the trees, the oceans and the seas, the mountains and the hilltops, the animals, the sun and the moon and the stars, the fire, air, water, and the four corners of the earth, and in your whole body you feel that this light is also love because it begins to heal everything in Creation. It now comes to be your turn to be filled with the light and love of God so that you too can receive His life and be renewed. You see God look upon you with eyes of love and you hear God speak to you and say, "This is your fill." You feel your whole body, your mind, your soul, and your spirit become filled with the light and the love that God poured into you so you could feel your oneness with God and all Creation. You feel your light become connected to everything. You feel this oneness as God places a part of the earth in your body, a part of the waters in your soul, a part of the air in your mind, a part of the fire in your heart, and a part of the ether in your consciousness. The more you believed in God, and accepted His gift, the more the love and light poured into you, and the deeper your connection to the Earth became, until you too could feel your power heal the Earth and all its creatures. This love purified you and the light made you wise. Thank you, Lord, Creator, for the gift of life you have given me. Thank you for giving me the gift of wisdom. Help me to love and accept myself and all people without conditions so that I can continue to shine the light of God and be the love of God in humanity. Help me to remain here, in your Heaven for an eternity, with you in everlasting peace. AMEN

Bibliography

A Precious Garland Of The Supreme Path, trans. by. Dr. Konchok Rigzen. Acarya Kundakunda's Pancastikaya-sara, Kundakunda, Pancastikaya. *Ashtavakra Gita,* http://www.holybooks.com/ashtavakra-gita/
Basal, Sunita Pan, *Encyclopedia of India.* Bhaktivedanta, A. C. Swami Prabhupada, *Bhagavad Gita.*
Bodhi, Bhekkha, *The Connected Discourses of the Buddha,* A New Translation of the Samyutta Nikaya, Wisdom Publications, Boston.
Confucius, *The Analects Of Confucius,* http://www.indiana.edu/~p374/Analects_of_Confucius_ (Eno-2015).pdf
D. D., Rev. J. Stevenson, *Kalpa Sutra,* London.
Dhammapada, *The Buddha's Path of Wisdom,* trans. by Acharya Buddharakkhita.
Diamond Sutra, by Dhyana Master Hsüan Hua, Buddha Dharma Education Association, Inc.
Cherng, Wu Jyh, *Daoist Meditation,* Sitting Dragon, 2014. Conway, Timothy, "This is All A Dream," 1983/2006.

Gleanings from the Writings of Baha'u'llah, Translated By Shoghi Effendi.

Hans-Georg Möller, *Zhuangzi's "Dream of the Butterfly," A Daoist Interpretation*, *Philosophy East and West,* Vol. 49, No. 4 (Oct., 1999), pp. 439-450.

http://www.spiritual-quotes-to-live-by.com/100-inspirational-native-American- quotes.html

https://www.uua.org/worship/words/quote/knowing-who-you-are

https://www.goodreads.com/quotes/659524-calm-and-repose-are-what-he-prizes-victory- by-force

http://www.unification.net/ws/theme082.htm

http://www.unification.net/ws/theme022.htm

Joseph Campbell and the Power of Myth - TV.

Krishnanada, Swami, *Chandogya Upanishad*, The Divine Life Society, India.

Lennon, John, http://www.keepinspiringme.com/john-lennon-quotes/

Lebkowicz, Lesley Fowler and Tamara Ditrich with Primoz Pecenko, Sutta Nipata, www.buddhanet.net/pdf_file/Sutta-nipataBM6.pdf

Lotus Sutra, Translated from the Chinese by Tsuganari Kubo and Akira Yuyama, Numata Center, 2007.

McKiel, Allen, *Beyond Tolerance*, Religion and Global Community, Interfaith Resources, 2007.

Nearman, Herbert, *Buddhist Writings on Meditations and Daily Practice: The Serene Reflection*, Shasta Abbey Press, 1994.

Pestell, Ben, *Translating Myth*, Routledge, 2016.

Plato, *The Collected Dialogues of Plato*, trans. By F. M.

Cornford, in, Ed. By Edith Hamilton and Huntington Cairns, Princeton: Princeton University Press.

Reps, Paul, *Zen Flesh, Zen Bones*, Tuttle Publishing; Reprint edition, 1998.

Schmaltz, David M., *The Blind Men and The Elephant, Mastering Project Work*, Berrett- Koehler Publishers; 1 edition, 2003.

Stories of Encounter: Pray Now Devotions, Reflections, Blessings and Prayer, edited by Hugh Hillyard Parker, St Andrew Press, 2017.

Sutra of Hui Neng, Translated by Thomas Clearly.

Sutra of the Great Accomplishment of the Maitreya.

Suzuki, Daisetz Teitaro, *Lankavatara Sutra.*

Theosophical Publishing Society, *Theosophical Sifting*, Volume 5, Nabu Press, 2014.

Vivekananda, Swami, *Raja Yoga*, New York Brentano's 1920.

Wiman, Christian, *My Bright Abyss: Meditation of a Modern Believer*, Farrar, Straus and Giroux; Reprint edition, 2014.

Zerah, Aaron. 365 Spirit: A Daily Journey For Your Soul.

Zen Sourcebook, Traditional Documents from China, Korea, and Japan, edited by Stephen Adiss, Stanley Lombardo, Hackett Publishing Company, 2008.